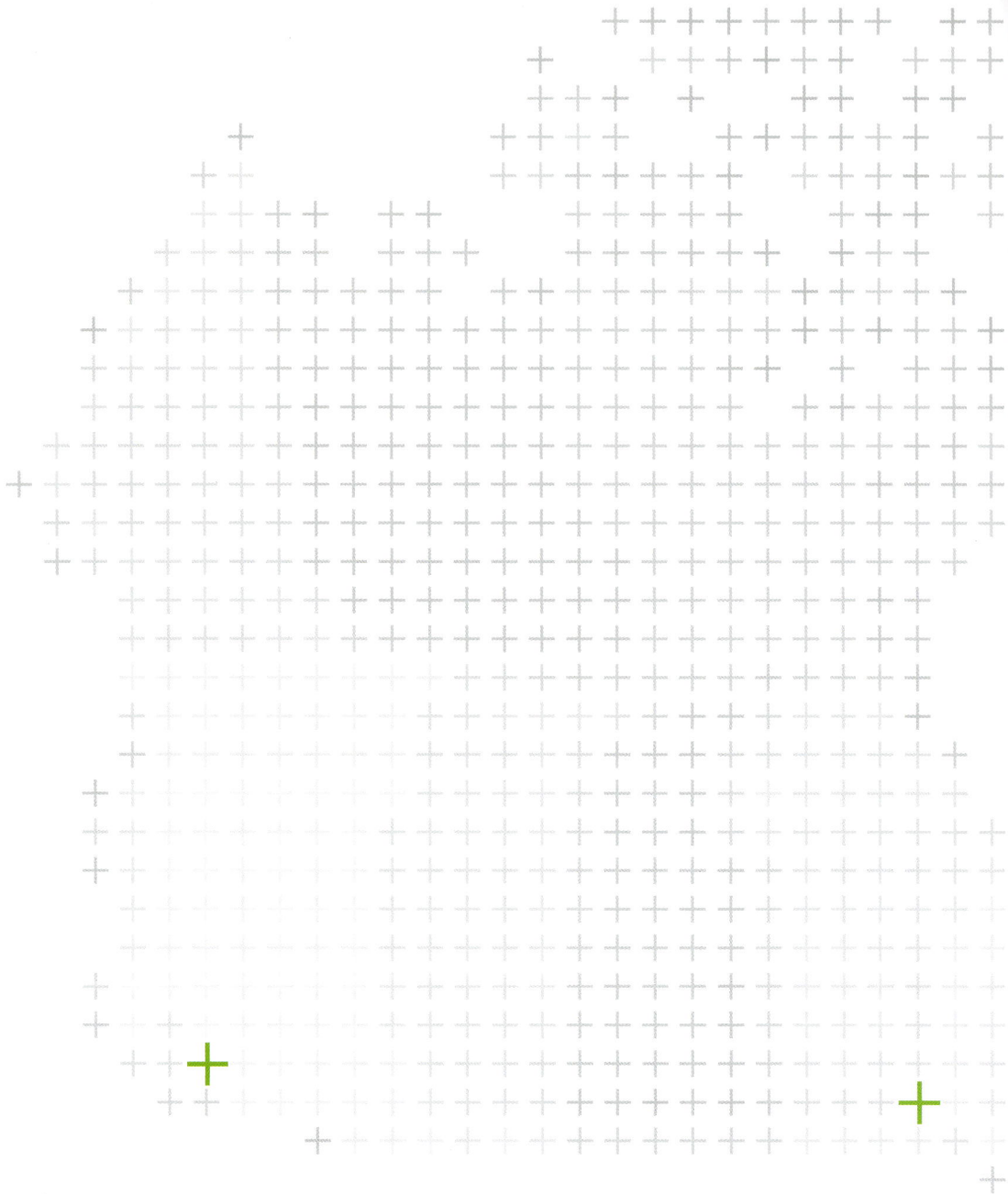

TWENTY + CHANGE

EMERGING CANADIAN DESIGN PRACTICES

02

edited by
Heather Dubbeldam
Lola Sheppard

Riverside Architectural Press

Twenty + Change 02

Editors: Heather Dubbeldam, Lola Sheppard
Production: Heather Dubbeldam, Farid Noufaily, Lola Sheppard, Rufina Wu
Design: Farid Noufaily, Rufina Wu
Copy-editor: Doris Cowan

Printing by Regal Printing Limited, Hong Kong
This book was set in Slate Std and Univers LT Std.

Publication & Coordination Committee:
Heather Dubbeldam, Cathy Garrido, Meg Graham, Trevor
McIvor, Cindy Rendely, Lola Sheppard, Scott Sørli

Special thanks to:
Joost Bakker, Johanna Bollozos, Ian Chodikoff, Anne Cormier, Andrew DiRosa,
Vanathy Ganesharajah, Lynden Giles, Leslie Jen, Naomi Kriss, Bindya Lad,
Heather MacMullin, Christine Macy, Kevin McIntosh, Thomas Nemeskeri,
Farid Noufaily, Chris Pommer, Mason White, Emma Wright, Rufina Wu

Special thanks to our sponsors:
Canada Council for the Arts, Royal Architectural Institute of Canada,
PCL Construction Leaders, Forbo Flooring Systems, Astley Gilbert
Limited, Blackwell Bowick Partnership Limited, Dunleavy Cordun
Associates Inc, Fowler Bauld & Mitchell Architecture, Ridley Windows
and Doors Inc., Velux Canada Inc., Manitoba Association of Architects,
Nova Scotia Association of Architects, Architectural Institute of British
Columbia, Festival of Architecture & Design, University of Waterloo
School of Architecture, Gladstone Hotel, Barzelle Designs Ltd.

Canada Council   Conseil des Arts
for the Arts   du Canada

Published with the generous assistance of the Canada Council for the Arts.

ISBN:978-1-926724-01-0

Contents

Preface

It was with great excitement that this year's curatorial committee learned of the broadening of Twenty + Change's mandate, an exhibition program created to showcase emerging architects, landscape architects and urban designers in Canada. Launched in 2007, Twenty + Change focused on emerging Toronto-area practices. The inauguration of this exhibition program generated considerable discussion amongst the Toronto design community that had been waiting for several years to witness a new generation of designers move the discourse of contemporary architecture forward. With Twenty + Change 02, we hope that the momentum behind the 2007 exhibition will continue as it supports emerging practitioners from coast to coast. In future iterations, we anticipate that all regions of the country will actively engage in the architectural discourse that Twenty + Change wishes to disseminate.

There was a general belief amongst this year's curatorial committee that it was difficult to select a vanguard group of twenty emerging designers who are currently leading the profession into the future—and one of "change." Our committee understood the meaning of the word "change" to be associated with "leadership" or "innovation." And while there are examples of firms that continue to evolve and mature their practices, we felt that many of today's emerging designers are producing derivative work where the aesthetic is heavily influenced by established and well-known Canadian firms. There are several reasons why this phenomenon exists. One explanation can be attributed to the fact that many of Canada's emerging designers worked in Canada's leading firms prior to establishing their own practices. Another reason is simply that it takes a seasoned practitioner to evolve away from dominant design trends of a particular region in this country. Notwithstanding the derivative tendencies, a deep appreciation for the landscape and a genuine concern for macro issues such as the environment were evidenced in many of the projects. These concerns will hopefully continue to be expressed by emerging practices as they explore and engage the public realm in meaningful ways.

The curatorial committee also observed that opportunities in Canada for new firms to test their ideas in practice are often lacking. For example, we noted the general lack of architecture competitions in Canada and relatively few opportunities for commissions involving a high level of custom-made, innovative work for young firms. Despite these constraints, these emerging practices exhibited an extraordinary level of entrepreneurship, many even going so far as initiating their own client group or seeking out innovative ways to fund their own projects. It appears that the traditional career trajectory of designing single-family dwellings for many years before being given the opportunity to take on larger public commissions is beginning to change as emerging practices are finding new opportunities in today's new market realities.

Amongst the firms selected for Twenty + Change 02, some were clearly more representative of the operative word "change" than others. Many of these firms convincingly recognized the importance of self-initiated commissions that live up to the curatorial committee's hopeful attitude towards future directions in the profession. For example, Urban Republic's Peeroj Thakre in Vancouver makes it a priority to extend the public's expectations of an architect's potential to impact and enhance public space. One of Urban Republic's notable projects includes a temporary drive-in theatre set atop a parking garage in Vancouver's Gastown. Also from Vancouver, mcfarlane | green | biggar ARCHITECTURE + DESIGN INC., has nurtured a successful business model since its inception in 2003 that relies on developing a niche in small regional airports—a formula that has also contributed to its rapid growth. Recognizing the importance of undertaking research and design in practice—specifically in the arena of strategic low-cost infill housing—has given the two-year-old Winnipeg firm of 5468796 Architecture Inc., a perceived edge in the marketplace. spmb, another Winnipeg-based firm, is focused on producing evocative installation art, such as its Table of Contents or its Plage installation. Toronto's Lapointe Architects' environmentally sustainable cheese factory in Prince Edward County offers a convincing example of the firm's ideals regarding sustainable design—a practice methodology that is perhaps its most valuable asset. Also from Toronto is Lateral Office. Founded in 2002 by Lola Sheppard and Mason White, Lateral Office's design work is highly engaged with the public realm. This is not surprising, given the two partners' academic commitments. Montreal's _naturehumaine presented some delightful interior projects expressing a conscious display of design rigour and intelligence. The other Quebec firm, Montreal's NIPpaysage, has quickly gained praise for its architecture and landscape projects in Montreal. Based in Saint John, New Brunswick, another inspirational practice is The Acre Collective who has produced several small-scale projects that display a rare sense of "delight".

The more successful firms in the exhibition are able to push the expectations of architecture, while encouraging their clients to expand their definition and scope of a meaningful architectural commission. The curatorial committee acknowledges the importance of Twenty + Change as an exhibition series that can raise the public's awareness of the quality of architecture being produced across the country.

Congratulations to all those selected and to other designers across Canada who continue to define and broaden the reach of architecture today.

Ian Chodikoff
April 2009

2009 Curatorial Committee

Anne Cormier graduated from the McGill School of Architecture and holds a C.E.A.A. Architecture urbaine from the Ecole d'architecture Paris-Villemin. She is a co-founder of Atelier Big City, a Montréal-based firm that has received numerous awards including three Governor General's awards, the Grand Prix for Order of Architects in Québec in 1994, and the Canada Council Prix de Rome in Architecture in 2006. Through her work at Atelier Big City, Anne has been involved with many landscape, urban design and architectural projects and competitions in Canada and internationally. Anne has taught in Canada and abroad, and is currently Director of the School of Architecture at the University of Montréal.

Christine Macy is the Dean of the Faculty of Architecture and Planning at Dalhousie University. Educated at UC Berkeley and MIT, she practiced architecture in New York and San Francisco before establishing her partnership, Filum, with Sarah Bonnemaison in 1990, specializing in lightweight structures and public space design for festivals. Before joining the faculty at Dalhousie, Christine taught at UC Berkeley and the University of British Columbia. Her research areas include the representation of cultural identity in architecture, public spaces, civic infrastructure, temporary urbanism, and festival architecture.

Chris Pommer is a founding partner in Toronto-based PLANT Architect Inc. PLANT is an interdisciplinary firm that branches into the domains of architecture, landscape, ecology, furniture, art, and graphic design. Synthesizing the insights and expertise of related disciplines, the practice responds to and embraces the increasing complexity of the world and the ambiguity of where landscape, built form, and design intersect. PLANT's integrated approach fosters a collaborative spirit, a multi-layered design solution and enriches each project with a fine grain of detail.

Joost Bakker is a principal of Hotson Bakker Boniface Haden architects + urbanistes in Vancouver. He studied economics and architecture at the University of Toronto and subsequently worked for George Baird who influenced Joost's interest in urban issues and the public realm. Through more than 30 years of professional practice, Joost has focused on innovative mixed-use, residential, institutional and cultural projects. He is co-author of many significant urban design and planning projects, including a landscape/public art commission for the Vancouver Olympics. Joost is active in the arts and civic politics in Vancouver and has mentored at the UBC School of Architecture.

Ian Chodikoff is an architect and the editor of Canadian Architect magazine. His professional interests focus on enabling mechanisms for social change at the urban scale, which include aspects of landscape and the public realm to new forms of commercial and residential development. His research focus includes the links between multiculturalism in the suburbs of Canadian cities, as well as transnational migration and its effects on urban development. Ian has lectured in various schools and cities across North America, served on numerous juries and has written in a variety of magazines and journals on issues ranging from planning to sustainability.

Introduction

Why is it that we hear more about young design firms from around the world than we do about rising firms in Canada? Perhaps it is the vastness of our country, or lack of venues dedicated to disseminating the work of emerging practices. Perhaps despite all the discussion of architecture in a globalized age, it is that, in Canada, our profession remains highly local. Whatever the reason, young Canadian practices are operating in local design contexts and there is little opportunity for understanding the diversity of work being produced across the country.

Twenty + Change began in 2007, with a focus on emerging Toronto firms in the disciplines of architecture, landscape architecture, and urban design. Based on the success of the exhibition and a recognition of the significance of this forum, a group of practices discussed the evolution of Twenty + Change. We quickly agreed to expand the scope Canada-wide, and to produce a publication that would serve as a record of the work, issues and approaches of this burgeoning generation of designers.

While Canada has its laurel for young architects in the form of the *Prix de Rome*, there is no venue – in the form of exhibition or publication - for disseminating the work of designers beyond the local or regional. Holland's *Maaskant Prize* is associated with a publication, the United State's *Young Architects Forum* (in which Canadians have been included for the past three out of five years) produces a publication, as does France's prestigious *Albums des Jeunes Architectes*.

In a sense, Twenty + Change's self-proclaimed mandate is to take on the role of disseminator, with both a degree of criticality and a spirit of inclusion. More mixed-tape than album, the intention of Twenty + Change is not to produce a publication of the three or five "best" firms in the country—indeed how would one define that—but rather, to give a sampling of the range of concerns and approaches, taking place across the nation.

The response to the Twenty + Change 02 "Call for Projects" was impressive—101 projects were submitted from firms in thirteen cities in eight provinces. The work submitted was a cross-section of projects of varying scales, theoretical and built, and exploring a range of ideas and common challenges facing us today. The curatorial committee, comprised of noted authors, educators and professionals, selected a group of twenty-one firms that they felt were producing work that addressed significant contemporary issues and opportunities: questions of how we produce and occupy the urban realm, new models for collective living addressing urban density and renewal, innovations in sustainability and material affect, the future direction of self-initiated commissions, the extension of an designer's potential to impact and enhance public space, and new models of practice, amongst others.

Twenty + Change 02 features these projects as a collection of emerging firms' work and includes texts written by each firm that describe their practice and the project(s) selected. Many of the contributing authors noted the significance of positioning one's work as an emerging designer. Architecture is a profession regulated by provincial bodies and legal codes, but its primary role is to act as a cultural and social agent, to question how we occupy our environments, whether urban or rural, domestic or public. The work included in Twenty + Change 02 takes on these questions with varying methodologies and intensity. We look forward to continue expanding the scope of Twenty + Change—both in its geographic reach and its design ambitions.

Heather Dubbeldam
Lola Sheppard

There is No Such Thing As Canadian Design

Alex Bozikovic

What is Canadian design? As Twenty + Change expands its scope from Toronto to cover the entire country, it seems inevitable to ask what binds all this work together. Yet no one seems eager to address the question—not the curatorial committee, not the architects and designers themselves.

And no wonder. Just asking it evokes fifty years' worth of hand-wringing about our national identity. The literary and cultural critic Northrop Frye suggested that the essential question for Canadians, isn't "Who am I," but rather "Where is here?" In an era where Canadians are designing behemoths in Dubai, Zaha is building in Vilnius and construction shots of the new Gehry are on everybody's iPhone, there's no singular answer. Instead, the response from the practices in Twenty + Change 02 is: wherever I am.

These designers work within a global conversation about architecture— and where their work displays a strong sense of place, it's local, not national. Buildings don't go up in countries, after all; they go up in cities and towns, places with their own culture, climate, geography, materials, building codes. There are regional influences that cross the US border. And all those particulars are more important for emerging architects, who often have to work in their own backyards.

Still, at first glance, there seems to be a common aesthetic language, forms and materials that are especially (though not uniquely) Canadian. This is a sign that this generation of practitioners has settled on a set of common idols; they largely draw from the more modest, humane strands of modernism, the legacy of Aalto, Kahn, Thom and Erickson. But then many of these projects, especially the best ones, offer dissenting views. Paul Raff's Cascade House, for instance, is all slate, bamboo, and channel glass. Natural materials, sure, but the way it faces off against the street—like a gorgeous, alien rock formation—belies any clichés about Canadian politeness.

The real common thread here is a set of shared ideas on the big questions: what architecture should do and what it should be about: 21st-century urbanism, seeking environmental sustainability and rethinking housing.

In Saint John, for instance, the Acre Collective makes a tiny wine-bar patio into a piece of sculptural urbanism, bringing street life to a somewhat forbidding masonry building. They are doing what young architects around the world are striving to achieve: using small interventions to reanimate districts and cities.

Other practices in bigger cities are already working on urban strategies at a larger scale. In Winnipeg, 5468796 Architecture Inc. have come up with bold solutions for infill development. A condo development dubbed YouCube brings a series of Bauhausian white cubes to a waterfront industrial site. A complex puzzle of units enables high density but also spatial variation, both in- and outside the units. And the cheekily named BGBX, which wraps courtyard apartments in a corrugated metal box, is a well-thought-out solution for an inhospitable site. It suits Winnipeg's climate and is a worthy heir to the city's visible modernist heritage – and at the same time, it's clearly connected to work from Chicago, Los Angeles and Rotterdam.

Some firms are designing entire neighbourhoods. Lateral Office proposes a flexible scheme for the redevelopment of an urban airfield in Reykjavik: airstrips, turned into linear green spaces, define mixed-use precincts, and the parks hold facilities for agriculture and energy production. Such creative solutions for disused sites will be crucial for the city of the next generation, determining its texture and how close it gets to achieving sustainability. It is not surprising that Lateral is in the thick of this debate. After all, the firm is based in Toronto, where the discussion around urban landscape is highly sophisticated (even if the reality lags behind). Field Operations and Michael van Valkenburgh are working here, and a local project, the unrealized OMA and Bruce Mau Design proposal for Downsview Park in 2000, had a formative effect on the large-parks debate. Lateral is not the only firm in the exhibition tackling such problems; similar issues play out in NIPpaysage's hundred-year management plan for Point Pleasant Park in Halifax, which looks at incremental strategies for renewing the landscape and use of this park devastated by Hurricane Juan.

The question of sustainability is addressed most directly on a smaller scale, by Lapointe Architects' Fifth Town Artisan Cheese Factory, which is literally built into its rural Ontario site. It uses a wetland to compost cheese-making waste, but also employs the latest in sustainable materials and technologies. And while its modernist architectural language may be unusual in the neighbourhood, it's very much in the spirit of a generation of work coming out of Toronto and Waterloo.

Many of the projects in Twenty + Change 02 are small-scale: single-family houses, country houses, and renovation projects. This is the traditional forum for young practices, and some of the examples here are excellent. Vancouver's Marko Simcic delivers two cottages that play off ideas of landscape (that old Canadian standby) in remarkable ways: on Vancouver Island, the Metchosin House's complex form is sculpted in part by the root system of the surrounding trees. Molly's Cabin, by Toronto's AGATHOM Co., combines aggressive form-making with the rustic vernacular of Ontario's Georgian Bay shore, which is connected to the cabins of New England, buildings deferring and responding in very direct ways to landscape.

In Toronto, Dubbeldam Design Architects puts a contemporary addition onto one of the city's iconic Victorian houses. It's a familiar and fairly modest task, but the results are fresh—both for the house's incorporation of passive sustainable strategies and the sophistication of its spatial and material details. And in Montréal, naturehumaine reinvents a classic triplex as a lofty single-family house. Inside, the architects contrast contemporary insertions with remnants of the existing exposed wood structure. Outside, with the front façade's two-coloured brickwork, they make playful contemporary art out of familiar local materials.

Another route for young practices is toward, literally, art—building their practices not strictly through construction (or "paper projects") but public artworks and interventions. Winnipeg's spmb, Lateral Office, and NIPpaysage have each entered creative work at the boundary of landscape design and public art. These are opportunities to flex creative muscles while remaining unbound by the demands of building. The poster children here are landscape architects North Design Office, whose Verdant Walk project in Cleveland sums up the most diffuse of the work in this exhibition—witty, sophisticated, not in any way recognizably Canadian.

On the other hand, some of the practices here are trying to achieve a broader relevance through architecture. Take Toronto's RVTR, whose Latitude Housing System is a scheme for sustainable housing in northern Russia. RVTR bill themselves as "creative problem-seekers," and with this project they are taking on a serious challenge: sustainable prefab housing—but, really, this work is global in its conception and its intent. Likewise RVTR's design for a "Post-Carbon Highway." The venue in this case is Canadian, the 401 highway across southern Ontario, but the challenge, reinventing overtaxed highways, will be everywhere tomorrow. It's exactly the kind of big-picture project that young designers should be seeking out. In Vancouver, Urban Republic finds another one: putting urban infrastructure to better use. Their Gastown Drive-In, with some brilliant lateral thinking, suggests how to make a gathering place out of a parking garage while it lies fallow at night.

The high standard of those projects isn't matched by everything in this exhibition; after all, this is the work of young practices. But as a group, these projects are remarkably diverse, many of them are original, and many of them take up the world-changing spirit of classic modernism. This makes it difficult to sum them up with an aesthetic or ideological catchphrase. You could argue that such diversity is what being Canadian is all about. Many critics and historians have tried this, not least with the field of architecture. Take the great generation of Canadian modernists: there wasn't much Canadianess unifying the 1960s work of, say, Thom and Moriyama. The best designers of that era—and the best of ours too—worked outside the constraints of a cultural agenda. This show's crop of designers seems likely to do the same, keeping their creative focus on the work at hand but their vision and imagination always open to the world at large.

On the Emerging Designer

David Theodore

We must think about a curious condition. A plethora of good talent, a plethora of bad design. This is the designer's dilemma today: to do good work in a culture inundated with bad design. This is the scene, the society, into which unknown designers must "emerge."

But must they emerge? No. Too often, we use the word "emerge," without reflection, when we wish to describe someone "starting out." I wish to better understand "emerge." For even though it's ingrained in the way we think about design careers, the concept of "emerging designer" is unhelpful, obscuring much more than it clarifies, mystifying apprenticeship as a ritual of the chosen. Even in the Twenty + Change exhibitions, the first in 2007 and second in 2009, the designers represented are not all simply "beginning." In Hollywood, a star is born. The pop star is an overnight success (ten years in the making). A lawyer is called to the bar. An architect emerges. What does it mean to emerge and how do you do it? What is the benefit of emerging? Why should we encourage emerging designers?

I have some thoughts on the matter. But other questions must be posed first. Why do we use "emerging" as a euphemism for "young, talented, and ambitious"? The notion is that the young designers of today will create the great designs of tomorrow. But we should know by now that youthful promise, though it may seem to augur success, is at best an undependable guide. History tells us that there are no prodigies in the traditions of architecture, landscape, and urban design, no designers equivalent to the five-year-old Mozart, fifteen-year-old Rimbaud, or teenaged Carl Friedrich Gauss. Yet we have an ongoing obsession with celebrating young, inexperienced-but-promising designers through exhibitions, magazine exposés, and books. Other professionals must think designers are batty. Imagine a book entitled "40 Dentists under 40," how absurd! Yet here we are, with Twenty + Change 02 returning to the field, once again bringing initiates into the light, as if we might at last secure the future of design.

Emerging, then, might be better understood as a simple name for a transitional career stage, for "starting out," for that awkward moment when you have left your internship (likely with a famous office) and have not yet stamped, signed, and sealed a building of your own. You emerge from obscurity when you take the first public steps on your way to establishing your name. But this, too, is false. Not all professional designers emerge. Because, after all, it is unnecessary to emerge. You can work for others. Or you can just do good work. Built work. You can follow in the footsteps of the Patkaus, Arthur Erickson, John B. Parkin, Nobbs & Hyde. You can be a good architect without emerging.

That is to say, "emerging" denotes something more than a transitional stage through which all architects' careers must pass. Although we use the term rather loosely today, the idea of emergence is based on a recent historical development concerning what constitutes good architecture practice. Only a particular kind of career should be thought of as emerging. Emerging architects develop a critical practice. It demands what academics call a "discourse" and vaudevillians a "schtick." You must have a way to talk about your work that, perversely, is not focused on design expertise, but rather orients your listener towards cultural, sociological, psychological, and philosophical problems. You can build a discourse. It does not have to be truly innovative; it can be a smokescreen. Discourse can be learned.

Some would say that in order to finish emerging, you have to build something. You cannot have a career with only a discourse. Otherwise your reputation will suffer. But again, this is false. It confuses the importance of establishing a professional practice with the notion of emerging as a designer. The confusion arises because we have that notion of critical practice. Why, behind the word "emerge," do we disguise this emphasis on "critical"?

The idea that designers should "build a critical practice" grew in response to modernist post-war challenges. Alongside a flirtation with hardcore functionalism and hardcore formalism, post-war educators promoted "emerging critical practice" as the model that would safe-guard the ideal of the designer as artist, of design as a fundamentally creative activity. The notion was an investment in the liberating poetic potential of the creative individual, a buttress and weapon against the de-humanizing drudgery of outdated building codes, grasping project managers, minuscule budgets, and societal indifference. The design education system continues to promote creativity. Why not empha-size other professional values, such as judgement, communication, or knowledge, to name just three? After all, designers today must confront a different set of challenges. They face problems forged in the smithy of postmodernism and the recent overreaction to the challenges of digital media: network theory, ecological disaster, globalization, information economies, all somehow portentously tied together by the internet.

Still, that's how design education wants to work: on the model of the creative individual. What was once a strategic response to a set of political and social conditions has been institutionalized into a grand transhistorical truth. Now "critical practice" has become the measuring stick for "innovative educators," dictating curriculum development, the types of problems that students are set, the types of skills they learn. The best professors—that is, the exciting teachers—are hyped as emerging designers with "critical practices." These practitioners remain hopeful that they can be professionals while still doing the kinds of projects originally conceived as school exercises: art installations or conceptual projects that "rethink" the city or "creatively engage" contemporary philosophy, or make "applied research" into Significant Issues in Society Today. Look around you, however. The projects in Twenty + Change prove the rule that most professional work isn't like this at all.

In fact, the model of individual "creative vision" probably does still work for art practice, which is essentially driven by state-funded grants and galleries (a system, by the way, in which all but a few artists are poor). And if you can characterize your architectural practice as "artistic"— that is, if you can get state funding—it can probably (and profitably) be characterized as critical. But that possibility only emphasizes that emerging practices are the exception; this is not how cities get built. Clients who will spend $2 million or $200 million rarely seek criticality in their designer or building; they seek professionalism. Exceptions are uncommon, which is why they seem valuable.

Moreover, today the design disciplines have a collaborative orientation. It's not just that teamwork is important, it's that architects and urbanists are now only part of a team, nothing more, rather than the master designers of the built environment. And at some point it must become clear even to architects, as it has to historians and theorists such as Henri Lefebvre and Michel Foucault, that architects long ago lost any authority over society's spatial order.

My viewpoint is warped by my years in Montréal, where you couldn't throw a brick without breaking a loft window belonging to a small, award-winning practice or Prix-de-Rome laureate. One would think that with so much poor design around—in our malls, in our suburbs, in our downtowns—there would be a huge push to hire these good designers. The fact is, there just isn't much work. Tim Horton's certainly isn't hiring them. Software mogul Daniel Langlois famously funds new media artists galore, but when it came time to design a prominent new building on Montréal's trendy lower Boulevard St.Laurent, did he hire one of Montréal's dynamic boutique firms? One whose offices are decorated with Governor General's Medals in Architecture? And did any of those emerging designers get a call when the city decided to develop new landmark Metro stations at Berri, Papineau, Frontenac? Just how is an emerging designer supposed to get a commission?

Indeed, "emerging" might be a more useful notion if there was a symmetrical category of "fading." The entire country, Canada's celebrated and vast expanse of mountains, lakes, and prairies, is simply overcrowded with emerging talent. But there are no exhibitions, alas, that celebrate the departure of designers whose turn on the stage is over, and who have graciously left for others the profiles in *The Globe and Mail* and the arts council application forms.

Québec, at least, mandates some design competitions for some public buildings. And for all the evil that competitions do, they also allow young designers, especially untested architects, access to some substantial commissions. And thus firms like Atelier Big City, Atelier In Situ and Atelier T.A.G. emerge. Granted, they may be no better off emerged than submerged; they seem to have no real chance of getting another commission unless they win another of those rare competitions. But so what? They have emerged! They have won the Prix de Rome! They have won national design awards! And thus one hears praise of competitions. . . we need more competitions. . . open competitions . . . anonymous competitions . . . even—just imagine it—paid competitions! What a concept: designers being paid to design!

This, then, is the elite community, the highest society, into which designers strive to "emerge."

At this point, we are ready for a short summary, some helpful tips, and some discussion of why—despite the drawbacks and confusion—it is wise to encourage "emerging," and why Twenty + Change is well worth the effort to organize, visit, and discuss. If you consider carefully the situation all-too-quickly outlined above, you'll see there really is no mystery in how to emerge. Here's the five-point plan:

1) Intern (with someone famous).

2) Teach (necessary if you are not independently wealthy).

3) Win an award or a competition or both (Sorry, posers, talent required).

4) Speak and publish, lecture and exhibit (anywhere you can).

5) Repeat numbers 2 to 4. This is now your life as an emerging designer.

There are simple ways to get your work talked about and, conversely, for you to talk about your work. You intern not just to learn the craft, but to connect with a network of people you can e-mail when a project develops. We often decry the superficiality of design magazines, but they are vital, community-building institutions. And you can easily get a magazine to publish your work. Do a project that photographs well. Then commission professional, beautiful photographs of it. Send them to magazine editors. Voilà.

The crucial point, then, is number 4. To emerge you have to speak and publish, lecture and exhibit. This is a peculiarity of a particular career path. I used to believe that only a combination of vanity and ambition emboldened callow designers to show off their first, formative projects. Montréal architect Gilles Saucier set me straight. He once outlined to me a vision of a community of Québec architects known internationally for their good design, in which his practice would have a place. Without such international awareness, his designs have no measuring stick, no comparables. I don't think his firm Saucier + Perrotte architectes are or ever were emerging; they chose a different way. But the lesson is still valid. He's not out there trying to crush the competition, but rather to build up and promote it.

And that's the irony of emerging. Self-promotion promotes the good of all. The audience for good work has to be built up. Slowly. The audience for your work also has to be built up. Speak and publish, lecture and exhibit. But remain mindful that "emerging" means more than "starting out," and might do more than initiate a select few into the elite. It means designers might participate, through speaking, writing, and teaching, in society. Looked at in this way, "emerging" is not just a career stage, it's a civic responsibility.

This, then, is the enlightened public, the community, which should be built when designers "emerge."

Twenty + Change 02
Projects

5468796 Architecture Inc.

Winnipeg, Manitoba

5468796 Architecture Inc. is a Winnipeg-based
studio established in 2007. The firm seeks to
challenge convention at all scales, from architecture
and design to detailing and engineering systems.

Believing that passion is contagious, that
great design need not be expensive, and that
it is possible to inspire even the most skeptical
client or contractor, 5468796 Architecture
Inc. views even the most mundane project as
an opportunity for creative exploration. The
studio welcomes chances to enhance design
debate among practitioners and promote public
awareness of architecture in Winnipeg.

In the past ten years the two principals, Sasa
Radulovic and Johanna Hurme, have spearheaded
several nationally and internationally recognized
architectural projects and competitions, and
continue to teach design at the Faculty of
Architecture, University of Manitoba. Current and
recently completed projects vary widely in scope
and scale, from furniture and storefront design to a
large hotel at the Winnipeg International Airport.

youCUBE
Winnipeg, MB

youCUBE is a housing development that explores the potential for density and affordability of a narrow, 264x63-foot urban lot. Located at the north end of a street currently being redefined by high-priced waterfront condominiums, the project occupies a seemingly unremarkable site, with limited visibility of the river, and neglected industrial surroundings.

The design places two-, three-, and four-storey townhouses in clusters on an elevated community plaza, with resident parking and a new driveway for vehicular access sheltered below. The plaza raises occupants above their industrial surroundings, capturing formerly inaccessible views and creating a permanent, communal space in a rapidly changing setting.

Each of the eighteen units is an open living cube defined by an architectural "wrap" that delineates floors, mezzanines, and storage units as it weaves through the space. The wrap reacts to and engages with the cube's vertical lines by folding back onto itself or traveling upward to form window openings with dramatic overlooks to the spaces below. Ceiling heights soar up to 36 feet, filtering daylight from the top level all the way to the ground floor. Touching only two walls at a time, the open edges of the wrap mediate between the simplicity of the building's shell and the complexity of the living arrangements within.

With all units arranged to capture views beyond the site's immediate context, and expansive public space for residents, youCUBE becomes an anchor point for a transitional area where history, industry, and small-scale housing have converged to face an uncertain future. The project has the potential to act as a catalyst for future growth, encouraging expansion of housing and the existing park system along the full length of the street.

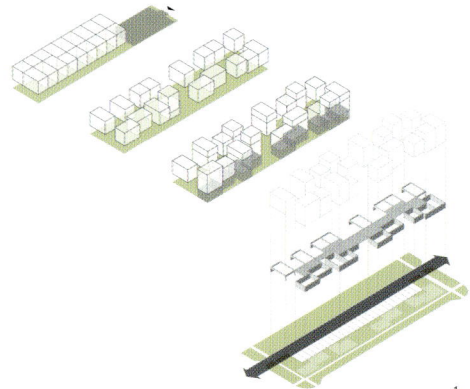

1

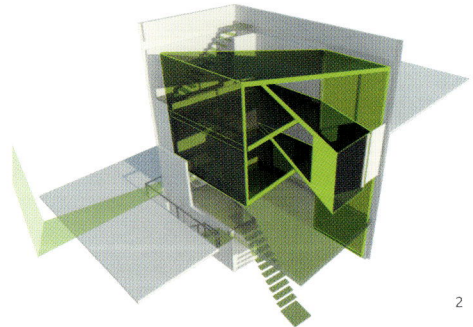

2

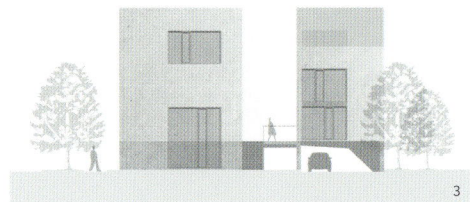

3

1   Individualized units are connected by an elevated plaza with parking below
2   X-ray view of typical unit interior wrap
3   Elevational relationship of units, plaza, parking and driveway
4   View of laneway with units on raised concrete foundation
5   A landscape of rooftop decks provide views of downtown and the river

5468796 Architecture Inc.

4

5

BGBX

Winnipeg, MB

Taking big-box typology as its initial metaphor, 5468796 Architecture Inc. transforms an existing parking lot on a desolate industrial corridor into a 26-unit housing development and public green space. The project begins as a white, nondescript box: a blank volume that is then strategically sliced at six points to reveal unexpected glimpses of lush foliage at the building's centre. This hidden realm opens up the box from the inside, creating a dynamic, multi-faceted facade. On the exterior, a corrugated metal skin shields residents from the harsh, unyielding character of the street. The courtyard invites residents to move past the building's hard edges into a place where the territory is less foreboding.

BGBX incorporates six separate blocks on its 355x97-foot lot. Each block has alternating two- and three-storey residential loft units and small-scale commercial flex spaces at grade. Vehicular access is off the public lane, and covered parking spaces are concealed from view beneath the eastern building block. All unit entrances are located off the courtyard at grade. These design elements ensure that the courtyard interior is animated solely by the lives of its inhabitants and the effect of changing seasons on the forest they overlook. Flexible spaces are accessible from the building's exterior to encourage commercial activity and a strong urban presence on the street.

The design of BGBX is simplified through the integration of its building systems; despite the project's irregular shape, a module based on hollow-core slabs four feet in width determines the entire architectural, structural, and mechanical composition of the units. In the courtyard, abundant vegetation acts as the lungs of the building, providing fresh air for residents. Grey water cisterns collect run-off from the roofs, and permeable surfacing and bioswales eliminate the need for catch basins.

1

2

1   Levels 1-3 floor plans with highlighted courtyard
2   Six irregular slices in the box invite street access to the courtyard
3   Conceptual image of the multi-faceted lush courtyard environment
4   Contrasting exterior of corrugated metal profiles
    and perforations over windows
5   Corten canopies, multi-faceted paneling and varied
    window patterns animate the interior court

5468796 Architecture Inc.

3

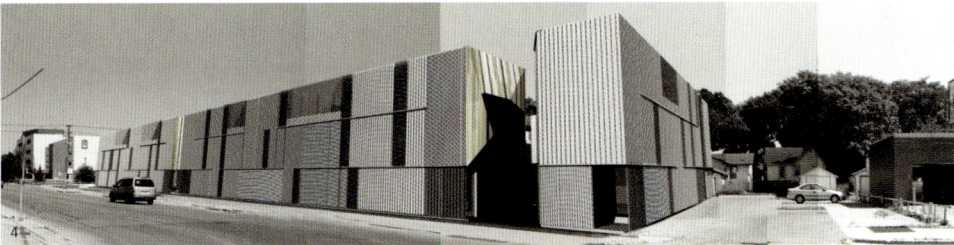

4

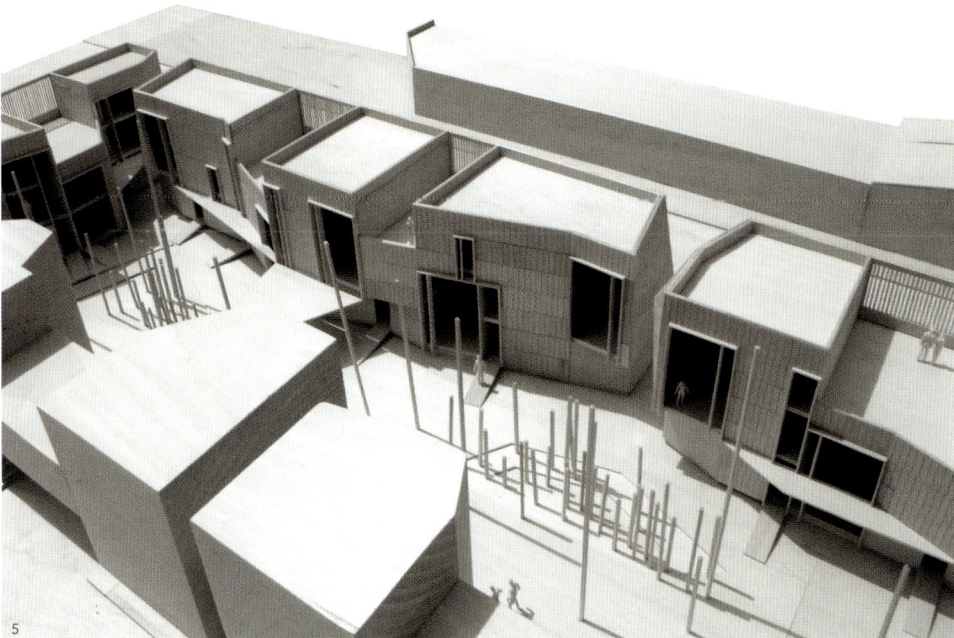

5

AGATHOM Co.
Toronto, Ontario

AGATHOM Co. is a Toronto-based architecture studio and workshop led by Adam Thom and Danish born Katja Aga Sachse Thom. After graduating together from SCI-Arc in Los Angeles, they moved to Toronto to start a family and set up AGATHOM Co. Their broad technical knowledge, dedication to craftsmanship and collaborative process all combine to create structures that are original and thought-provoking. The work of the award-winning studio is characterized by a unique fusion of sculptural form, landscape and durable architecture. They seek, through their work, to surprise and delight the senses while solving difficult programmatic problems.

Molly's Cabin
Pointe au Baril, ON

Three and a half hours north of Toronto, Pointe au Baril is in a remote archipelago in Georgian Bay —a large area of exposed Precambrian rock on a cusp of the Canadian Shield. Molly's Cabin is built on a 2.8-acre island, eight miles from the marina.

The aim of the project was to create a private seasonal retreat for a multi-generational family, balancing comfort with the bare necessities so that its inhabitants can live lightly on the land and fully engage with their surroundings. The 1,000-square-foot cabin consists of a bedroom, a living room with a library nook, a kitchen/dining room and a small loft that can serve as a drawing studio, library, playroom or supplementary bedroom. Although open in plan, the L-shaped design facilitates both privacy and interaction. Wooden decks and bridges extend the interior to the outdoors. Modernist architectural ideals inform the design, but also offer a playful reinterpretation of the humble architectural vernacular of these islands.

Shielded behind a large rock and a signature tree, the cabin fits snugly against the boulders, close to the edge of the water. The sweeping tent-like flaps of the asphalt-shingled roof provide both shelter and multiple views of the changing weather. Constructed from recovered timbers, and anchored by a Rumford fireplace made of local stone, the building was designed with plenty of dual function: exposed rafters provide storage, a dining-room cabinet doubles as an outdoor tool shed and the library windows roll open to convert the interior into a breezeway. Solar panels power a pump that draws fresh water from the lake. Propane and lamp oil fuel the stove, refrigerator, and lamps.

Molly's Cabin is familiar and experimental, respectful and assertive. The design challenges the current tendency in the area for extravagant architectural statements, creating a solution that is inventive and sustainable.

1   South elevation
2   East elevation
3   Living room view west to open water and anchoring rock
4   Living room and breezeway with dining room beyond
5   Night on the island
6   Back channel view

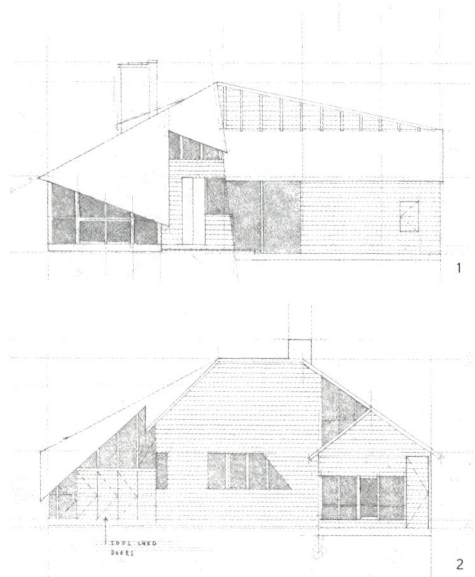

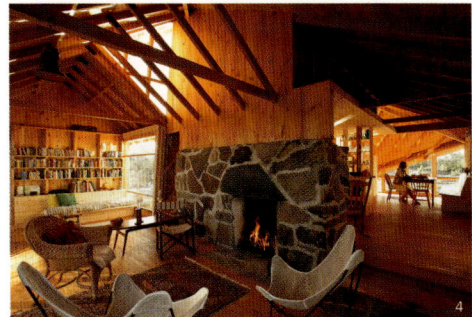

1

2

3

4

AGATHOM Co.

5

6

Altius Architecture Inc.

Toronto, Ontario

Altius is a full-service architecture and
construction management firm that
spearheads a larger collective of engineers,
consultants and constructors who share a
common goal: the creation of exceptional and
environmentally sustainable architecture.

 The firm is committed to a team approach to
building, believing that successful projects begin
with a confluence of architecture, structure,
mechanical systems and building technology.
An emphasis on working closely with our clients,
respecting the diverse beauty of Ontario's
landscape, and meeting the challenges of building
on unique sites has brought Altius a range of
projects, including Eels Lake Cottage. From its
inception, the practice has demonstrated a desire
to move beyond traditional practice by remaining
closely involved with the construction process,
to the point of offering complete construction
management services. This approach means
that the designers can see projects through
from start to finish, ensure consistency and
continuity, and achieve results that are beautiful,
sensitive, affordable, and sustainable.

Eels Lake Cottage

Apsley, ON

This lakeside residence takes advantage of topography, views and orientation to provide large, bright and open living spaces, indoors and out. Sustainable building techniques, both passive and active, guided the design process. The form and placement of the residence are a carefully considered response to the existing conditions at the Eels Lake site. The side-split massing mimics and is deliberately nested into a break in the topography of the underground rock. This use of the natural context minimizes the presence of the building while lifting the key living and master bedroom spaces upward for views and light.

The client required a design that kept personal living spaces separate from areas used for entertaining guests. One large, simple roof plane delicately joins these two programs; the public areas are contained within a glass volume. The private bedrooms are defined by the wooden insertion at the opposite side of the building. The side-split planning of the levels hinges around a central fireplace mass, with the 14-foot-high kitchen and dining space on one side and the more intimate living quarters and master suite on the other, raised a half-storey up to afford a view of the lake.

Among the sustainability features are natural ventilation, passive cooling, natural daylighting, a high-performance envelope design, passive solar heating, and advanced geothermal systems. Materials and finishes are renewable and nontoxic; appliances are low energy and water conserving.

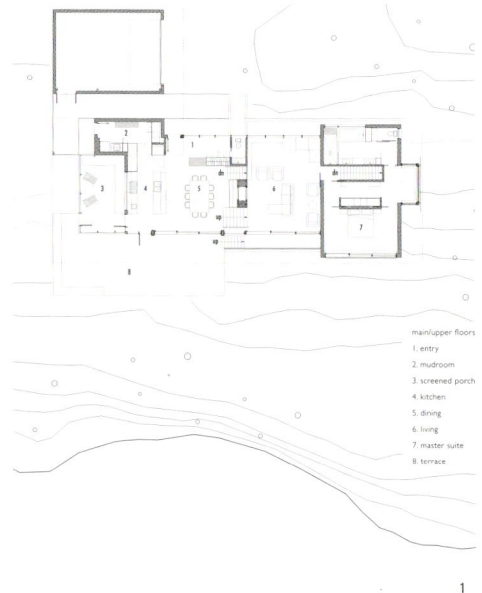

main/upper floors

1. entry
2. mudroom
3. screened porch
4. kitchen
5. dining
6. living
7. master suite
8. terrace

1

1   Site plan
2   Double-sided slate fireplace
3   Night view of floating roof through forest
4   Winter lakeside view
5   Simple massing under continuous roof plane

Altius Architecture Inc.

Campos Leckie

Vancouver, British Columbia

Campos Leckie is an interdisciplinary design studio based in Vancouver. The partnership was formalized in 2008 after several years of collaborative work by Javier Campos and Michael Leckie, both graduates of the University of British Columbia School of Architecture.

The office engages in design at a variety of scales and in a range of media including architecture, branding, and communication design. Its methodology is founded on the relationship between the opportunities afforded in the material aspects of a project and a disciplined engagement with the internal logic of the design. Committed to a rigorous process of discovery, the practice is centred on a deep-rooted fascination with the act of making.

Zacatitos 001

Los Zacatitos, Baja California Sur, Mexico

This project is the first of three desert dwellings, conceived as prototypes for off-grid living in a relatively extreme climate. All three research sites are located at Los Zacatitos, in a remote part of Baja California Sur, Mexico.

The minimal formal expression of the project was developed through a subtractive methodology applied to a series of carefully placed volumes. Mirroring the desert context, the understated formal complexity of the project was a direct response to extreme environmental conditions.

The project's four detached buildings and their related exterior spaces are arranged around the contours of a natural bowl on the four-acre site. Care was taken to locate them to catch prevailing breezes and allow seasonal arroyos (watercourses) to flow freely; their design was conceived in response to existing granite outcrops and the desert flora. Two smaller villas with sleeping accommodation flank the principal living space, and a garage/utility structure placed behind these buildings forms an entry court. Each of the two sleeping villas is organized around a courtyard planted with indigenous vegetation and irrigated with grey water. These passive heating/cooling strategies are founded on traditional Spanish architectural use of open-air courts, abstracted to create a modern green building form. The orientation of the villas, combined with the interrelationships of exterior circulation, interior and exterior living spaces and breezeways, use the Venturi effect to capture the prevailing breezes and to generate a comfortable living environment year round, while also mediating architectural considerations of privacy and place.

villa principal ①
villa oeste ②
villa este ③
garage ④
pool ⑤
bridge ⑥
solar panels ⑦
courtyard ⑧

1

1   Site plan
2   Villa este
3   Stair to roof deck
4   Villa principal - entry
5   Villa principal - pool and courtyard

Campos Leckie

D'Arcy Jones Design Inc.

Vancouver, British Columbia

D'Arcy Jones Design (DJD) is a small, young design practice with projects that fall primarily in the category of single-family dwellings. Within the admittedly prosaic realm of the suburban house, the partners' ambition is to develop tectonic strategies that question the familiar, while subtly transforming it into something fresh. An evolving language of contrasts, between the robust, heavy and sculptural on one side, and the transparent, light and minimal on the other, is carefully composed around the inventive use of common materials. Continuous research into products' potential and limitations, and close relationships with the people who commission and build each project, complement the office's formal design explorations.

Within a project's programmatic, geographical, and regulatory requirements, DJD seeks out peculiarities that can serve as motifs or design parti, allowing a gradual evolution of type. Whether it is a particularly difficult site, a conflict between a building code constraint and a client's needs, or simply the desire to capture a spectacular view, these peculiarities imbue the mundane with purpose. Moreover, the effect of such specific purpose on the firm's developing idiosyncratic architectonic language is not one-sided; the two influence each other in new ways with each new project.

The objective is to produce thoughtful, optimistic buildings that are contextually logical, astute, and critical. DJD considers a project to be successful when its beauty, generosity, and animation result from the continuous conversation between form and site, space and climate, user and enclosure; where the experiential qualities of a space are made tangible by the articulation of conceptual ideals in relevant and visceral ways.

Anderson House
Saltspring Island, BC

The undulating topography of this project's site feels remote , even though it is surrounded by suburban houses on bulldozed sites. The small, two-bedroom house is simultaneously grounded in and suspended over a rocky bluff, with panoramic views in all directions. The client's requirement for a single-storey house resulted in the diagrammatic concept of a heavy concrete plinth with an attached wooden springboard cantilevered out into the trees. The public living spaces suspended in the air have intimate views of treetops and expansive views of the ocean beyond, while the private spaces on the concrete plinth have compressed views of rocks and moss. The visceral experience of stepping from dense concrete onto hardwood flooring as one moves from the private to public spaces is exaggerated by the real sense that the ground is falling away beneath the building.

Unified under a simple roof form, the linear arrangement of spaces opens up at the centre—circumventing the local zoning requirement that disallows covered breezeways—to connect two living spaces. When the sliding doors of the "indoor" hallway are left open in the summer, the guest wing functions as a separate building. Notched skylights over the kitchen and breezeway legibly split the roof's knife-edged form into three segments, articulating the gaps between the functional zones with slots of strong light.

Rough concrete walls between the master bedroom and the guest wing improve privacy between the guests' and host's bedrooms, while their thermal mass acts as a heat sink. Combined with carefully placed operable windows and deep eaves on the south elevation, this house will be passively heated during the winter and cooled during the summer.

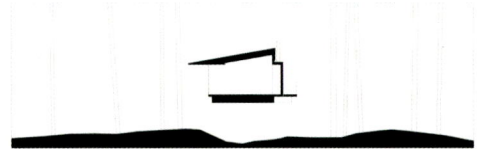

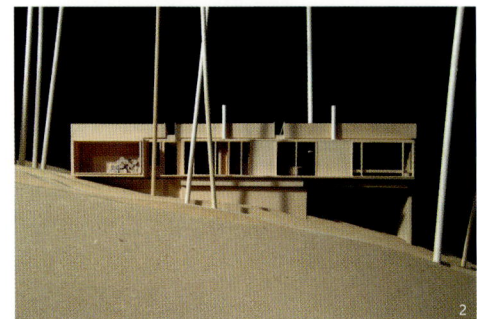

1   Sections
2   View from the north
3   View from the south
4   Breezeway and reflecting pool

D'Arcy Jones Design Inc.

Ernst-Ongman House

Whistler, BC

Perched on the side of a steep mountain, this dwelling is in an established neighbourhood near the Whistler–Blackcomb ski resort. The subterranean garage and house step up the craggy, rocky slope from the road, offering a weaving path from the wet forest floor up into the treetops.

The house's formal strategy is simple: a rough concrete plinth abstracts the region's rock outcroppings, supporting a primary framework of glulam beams. Budget constraints limited the amount of exposed structure, so the seismic piers and exposed beams were all carefully located to convey the layout of the house.

Forms carved from the simple two-storey form are clad in raw steel, already rusting even though the house is not quite completed. Windows are not detailed as punched openings, but are articulated as the voids between roof, walls, and floor. Inspired by the black-brown bark of trees on the site, exterior walls enclosing private spaces are clad in rough dark-stained cedar. The glow of the translucent channel-glass entry was conceived as an abstracted panel of ice during winter, and like the glow of a shoji screen in warmer seasons.

The master bedroom and the main living spaces are linked with an anodized aluminum curtain wall, blurring the two-storey separation and distinguishing the master bedroom from the guest bedrooms hierarchically. All other openings will have black aluminum frames, invisibly recessed into the dark siding.

To allow light and melting snow deep into the lower level, the upper-level deck near the barbecue will be a galvanized steel grate, typically used for ski lodge entrances.

To suppress the mass of the garage, native plants will be grown on the roof. A geothermal heating system will allow the house to be completely self-sufficient, with no outside energy used for heating or cooling. The concrete walls act as a thermal mass, balancing extreme day-night temperature fluctuations in this harsh winter environment.

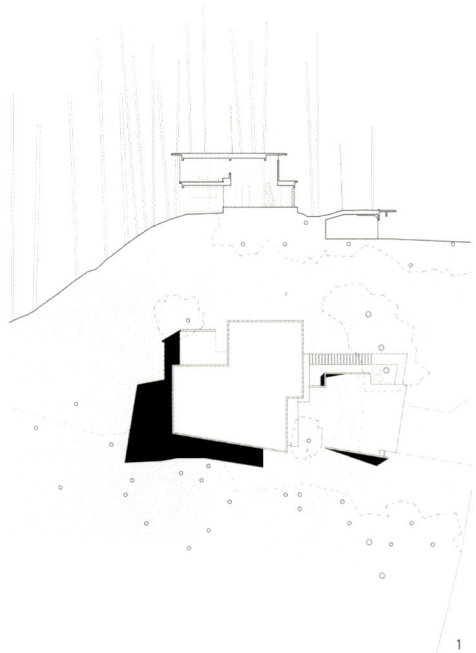

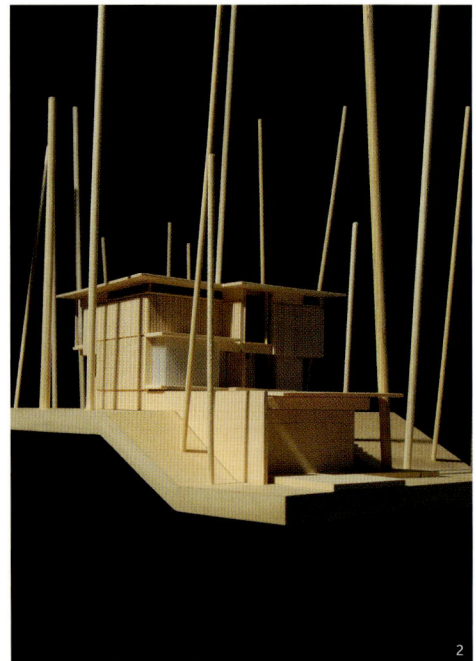

1   Site plan and section
2   Model from north
3   Interior perspective of living area
4   View from east ravine
5   View from south

D'Arcy Jones Design Inc.

3

4

5

Dubbeldam Design Architects
Toronto, Ontario

Dubbeldam Design Architects (DDA) was founded by
Heather Dubbeldam as a multidisciplinary practice
with a focus on contemporary design. In addition
to a broad range of professional experience in
architecture, the practice's portfolio includes interiors,
landscape design, lighting and furniture design.

Operating in a studio setting, the firm takes a
collaborative approach to projects and pursues
a rigorous level of detail and craft. From the
conception of each project through to construction,
the architectural team maintains a high degree of
involvement with consultants and contractors to
ensure tight control of project quality and detail.

Advocating the use of sustainable building practices as a
matter of course, DDA strives for an innovative approach
to all aspects of their work, including experimentation
with building materials, building form, and spatiality.
Without any preconceived style or convention, each
project is derived from its unique context and conditions.
The result is a diverse range of projects that emphasize
the specific needs and aspirations of the client, while
expressing the design approach of the practice.
In addition to receiving the Ontario Association of
Architects Best Emerging Practice in 2008, the practice
has received recognition through provincial and national
design awards, and through the publication of its work.

It is DDA's objective to produce architecture of
the highest quality while maintaining a life/work
balance. Exposure to external ideas and influences,
whether they originate locally or internationally,
generates new thinking and a fresh approach
to the design of the practice's projects.

Cabbagetown Residence
Toronto, ON

The renovation and renewal of this 100-year-old home in Toronto's Cabbagetown neighbourhood presented a challenge typical of this city—the updating of a house in a heritage neighbourhood, adapting the existing urban fabric while preserving its historic character. The Victorian front façade and side walls of this narrow semi-detached house were preserved, but the interior and rear façade were completely redesigned and rebuilt to counter the containment of the original Victorian plan. A modern renovation and addition were inserted into the historic shell, providing the house with passive sustainable technologies and materials, natural light, and an improved layout that supports the owners' love for entertaining.

Although small in area, the interior feels simultaneously compact and spacious. The reworked layout has an unexpected sense of fluidity, airiness, and access to natural light, achieved by an open-riser stair and an open plan. Various spaces are connected vertically and horizontally, yet still convey subtle demarcations of function through changes in floor heights, partial walls, or built-in furniture elements. The openness facilitates the movement of air throughout the house, allowing for passive natural cooling when the new operable windows are open. A long skylight above the staircase draws natural light down into the heart of the house, and significantly reduces the need for artificial lighting.

On each floor there are connections to the outdoors, inviting fresh air and an awareness of the changing seasons to pervade the interior. The attic was enlarged to accommodate a master bedroom with an adjoining bathroom, opening onto a sheltered roof deck that recalls a tree house. The second floor library is bathed in natural light from a full wall of glass, and in the kitchen an over-sized glass door slides open to a low-maintenance deck garden, allowing guests to spill outside in the warmer months.

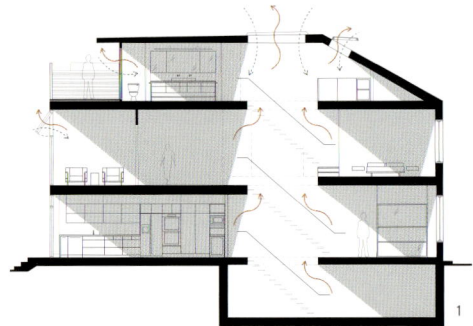

1   Section showing natural ventilation created by new
    operable skylights and specifically-located windows
2   Light-coloured materials in the kitchen help to
    reflect natural light into the narrow house
3   View of the library on the second floor
4   Victorian facade of house is preserved
5   New facade and addition on rear of house facing laneway
6   View of entertainment room with open riser stair
7   View into ensuite bathroom through to roof deck beyond

EVOKE International Design Inc.
Vancouver, British Columbia

EVOKE International Design Inc. was formed in 2001 by David Nicolay and Robert Edmonds. The practice combines conceptual thinking, building design, and interior and graphic design to ensure a consistent and coherent environment for each client. Projects have included residences, restaurants, hotels, and retail establishments. EVOKE has successfully branded and opened two restaurants of its own, Habit Lounge and the Cascade Room in Vancouver. The partnership has also launched a line of T-shirts and created concert street posters for Live Nation in Vancouver and New Orleans. Furniture and lighting prototypes are currently in development.

The company's guiding aesthetic principle is that an overall concept must be all-consuming in order to be successful. Corporate identity, signage, and graphics must not only complement, but also challenge and inform the interior/exterior design of an environment. Conversely, that interior design must have the ability to enhance communication between space and object. It is these two aspects that must go hand in hand in the design and execution of a successful branded environment.

W9 Houses

Vancouver, BC

The proposal is a plan for two houses on adjacent standard lots in the Point Grey neighbourhood of Vancouver, an RS-1 "outright approval" zoning district. In RS-1 areas, single-family residential projects are, in effect, guaranteed approval because the city wishes to maintain the residential character for the district while preserving outdoor space and views.

The challenge was to create a unique aesthetic for each house, despite the required economy of scale and similar floor plans. In addition, the houses were to be reflective of current design directions and technologies, utilizing green practices and materials. Finally, the objective was a plan that "lives large" despite the restrictive floor area and building envelope allowances.

In many cases, new houses built in this district are designed to mimic the historical aesthetic of the neighbourhood, but with lower-quality materials and detail. Often, two adjacent houses are virtually identical, and are simply "mirrored" on their sites to create a minimal sense of individuality. Evoke International's approach was to differentiate the façades through the use of materials (zinc, wood panels, stone, and cedar), massing and the placement of the windows. Both houses maintain the streetscape's scale, landscaping, and privacy. Open planning and a minimum of single-use rooms give the 2,000-square-foot floor plans a sense of spaciousness, and fluidity of movement from inside to outside.

The City of Vancouver's Building By-law Amendments for Green Homes meant that the W9 design was able to incorporate many green strategies, including sustainable exterior materials (zinc cladding, Prodema wood panels, natural stone, certified red cedar), polished concrete floors, low VOC interior finishes, and plans for the future installation of solar panels and an electric car charging system.

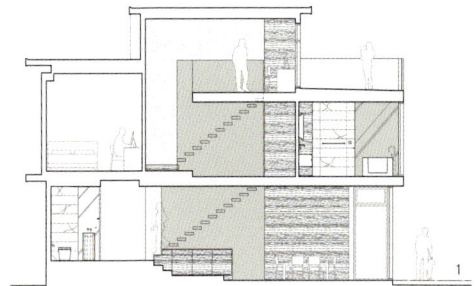

1

2

1   Section / interior elevations
2   Perspective elevation view from rear yard
3   Streetscape
4   Plans
5   Site Plans

EVOKE International Design Inc.

4

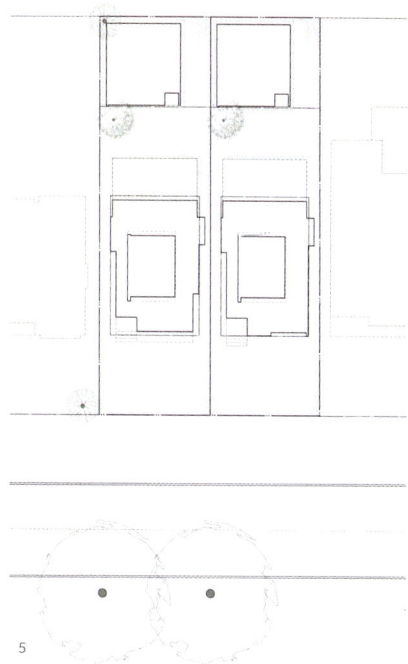

5

Gow Hastings Architects Inc.
Toronto, Ontario

Gow Hastings Architects Inc. is a Toronto-based architecture and interior design firm founded in 2002 by partners Valerie Gow and Philip Hastings. The firm specializes in creating vocational spaces for colleges and universities that simulate real-life scenarios.

Gow Hastings Architects Inc. unites comprehensive services with a flexible, creative approach. Projects are the result of a process rooted in inquiry, collaboration, and a constant search for new solutions to familiar problems. The firm's objective is to translate the unique personality and ideals of the institution into physical form, while also enhancing functionality and addressing the broader physical context. Purposeful and playful, projects celebrate clarity of form, proportion, clean lines, refreshing materiality, and imaginative use of colour and light.

Gow Hastings Architects Inc. considers its projects successful when each detail has purpose and integrity, when the overall impression reflects the spirit of the institution, and when the user is inspired by an encounter with the designed environment, ensuring spaces that please and sustain over time.

Humber Students' Federation

Toronto, ON

On the edge of a large atrium that is the hub of Humber College's main campus, the newly renovated office of the Humber Students' Federation is distinguished by a two-storey curtain wall of translucent and red-hued glass overlayed with a pattern of frosted dots. Up close these provide some privacy and visual interest. From a distance the dots convene to form a forest of trees from the adjacent Humber Valley –bringing an awareness of the surrounding nature to a space that lacks any views of the outdoors.

Prior to the renovation of the Students' Federation, the atrium lacked a clear focal point. The curtain wall now creates a coherent and visually stimulating backdrop for major events such as convocation and award ceremonies, and serves as a beacon for the organization's programs and services.

The upper floor of the Students' Federation is organized around a central glazed corridor with administrative offices on one side and a boardroom, communications suite, and lounge on the other. Beginning with the reception desk and continuing in the flooring, a long band of dark stained maple millwork leads down the corridor, weaving in and out the rooms, transitioning and transforming into a bench, shelf, and cabinets. The lower level, still under construction, will house games rooms, a programming suite and club offices.

Concerns for the office's indoor air quality, occupant comfort, and durability were key in choosing finishes. Products including engineered hardwood flooring, carpet, and marmoleum have high percentages of recycled and renewable content, with the latter two being recyclable. Additionally, all lighting fixtures are non-incandescent, and natural daylight from skylights pervades the entire area, filtering through the curtain wall from the adjacent space.

1   View of Humber Students' Federation Offices from the main corridor
2   Entry and reception area beyond
3   View of the waiting area through the curtain wall
4   Student lounge in front of the coloured and patterned glass curtain wall
5   View of the conference room and corridor

Gow Hastings Architects Inc.

Canadian Centre for Culinary Arts and Science

Toronto, ON

The recently completed Canadian Centre of Culinary Arts and Science at Humber College in Toronto included two kitchen labs, a wine-tasting lecture theatre, change rooms and washrooms, a food distribution centre, and corridors lined with display cases. The college's objective was to transform an under-utilized space into a dynamic centre of excellence for aspiring chefs.

The kitchens incorporate state-of-the-art technologies, such as induction cooking and a stainless steel ventilation and lighting ceiling system with unimpeded sightlines. Also included is a folding partition that enables the two labs and wine-tasting theatre to operate as separate classrooms or, when the partition is removed, as one large presentation space suitable for cooking competitions and television broadcasts.

With vast arrays of equipment, and strict requirements for function and hygiene, a culinary laboratory requires careful attention to detail to ensure that the many complex elements are combined into a uniform whole.

The two spaces are differentiated by material and texture to indicate their unique operation. In the kitchen labs, hard, impervious surfaces—stainless steel and bright, washable ceramic tile—were required to allow meticulous cleanliness. In contrast, warm, textured materials including iron spot brick, clear-stained oak panels, and red leather seating create a comfortable ambience in the wine-tasting theatre. Custom oak desks were equipped with integral lighting to allow students to evaluate the colour of the wines being served.

Seating was constructed from recycled leather, and products and finishes with low toxicity were specified throughout the project. Robust materials and details, including seamless safety flooring with integral coves and custom stainless steel counters, cabinets and shelves, will extend material life cycles and ensure that this heavily used facility will stand the test of time.

1   Main entry with views of the culinary labs through the slot windows
2   Interactive culinary lab with ventilated ceiling above
3   View of the demonstration counter and video monitors beyond
4   Wine lab and culinary labs open into one large space
5   Slot windows along the main corridor reveal the activity within
6   View of the wine tasting lab

Gow Hastings Architects Inc.

Lapointe Architects

Toronto, Ontario

Established in 2001 by Francis Lapointe, Lapointe Architects is dedicated to promoting environmental consciousness and cultural community through architectural innovation and sustainability. Lapointe grew up in Wawa, Ontario, where his passion for utilitarian and green building design was shaped by Northern Ontario's spectacular wilderness and the local forestry and mining industries. He graduated with a diploma in architectural technology from Centennial College, a bachelor's degree in architecture from Laval University, and a post-professional master's of architecture from the TUNS (now Dalhousie University). He has been a LEED Accredited Professional since 2005 and is an active member of the Canada Green Building Council.

The firm encourages clients to commission projects based on the LEED™ (Leadership in Energy and Environmental Design) and Green Globe rating systems. The recently completed Fifth Town Artisan Cheese Factory is the first LEED Platinum industrial building in North America. Lapointe also teaches environmental studies and LEED courses for Centennial College's Sustainable Architecture program.

Fifth Town
Artisan Cheese Factory

Prince Edward County, ON

Located in Picton, Ontario, the Fifth Town Artisan Cheese Company is a niche producer of fine handmade goat and sheep's milk cheeses. The facility, which was developed in a close collaboration between Lapointe Architects and the company's founder, is open to the public for retail sales, tastings, and educational purposes. On the model of a winery, visitors can observe and learn about both artisanal cheese and contemporary, sustainable architecture.

The building's orthogonal volumes are rendered in a modernist vocabulary of corrugated steel, concrete block, and wood. On the interior, crisp production areas contrast with the warmth of the retail and office spaces, which are defined by exposed wood trusses, natural floors, and a rich palette of colours, complementing the views of the surrounding rural landscape.

Ground source geothermal heat pumps, normally used to simply heat a building, are here used also to cool the structure and its many refrigerators. Excess whey, sanitary waste, and production wash water are treated in a constructed wetland on the property in a way that is not harmful to the environment.

The most significant design innovation was to "fold over" cheese production's conventionally linear process into a contained area behind a large glass wall. This design addresses the client's desire to open the manufacturing process to the public, while ensuring that all government regulations are met. Both the cheese-making process and the facility are cost effective, energy efficient, and totally "green"; Fifth Town is the first LEED Platinum industrial building in North America.

The meticulousness of the design reflects the quality of the cheeses. Fifth Town highlights how architectural innovation can combine with traditional food production techniques to create a model of community, environmental sustainability and social responsibility.

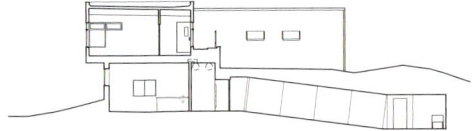

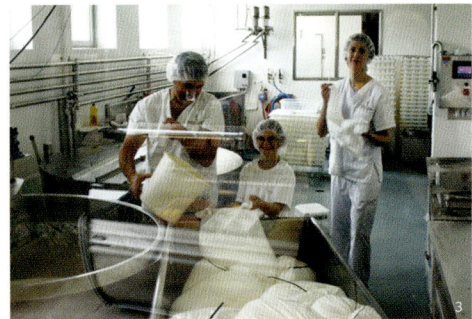

1   Section through production area and aging cave tunnel
2   Subterranean aging caves with large wheels of ripening cheeses
3   View into cheese production process
4   Environmentally-friendly Durisol block set against lumber
5   East elevation with view of aging cave tunnel
6   South-facing 'tasting' courtyard

Lateral Office

Toronto, Ontario

Lateral Office was initiated in 2002 by Lola Sheppard and Mason White, and is centred on a belief that architecture is an exercise in lateral thinking, and design is an empirical process inclusive of exterior environments, landscapes, and urbanism. Lateral embraces architecture as the interplay of dynamic spaces formed out of and responsive to a site's environment and history. Their design and research work explores Architecture as a by-product of complex networks within ecology, culture, and forms of urbanism.

The practice pursues projects at various scales within the public realm. Several projects have explored marginal, generic, and overlooked spaces. In such contexts, the objective is not to introduce foreign elements but rather to adapt and respond to existing ones, allowing the practice to test the limits and validity of ideas.

Lateral has won or been shortlisted for several international competitions in the United States, Canada, England, and Iceland. Lola and Mason received the Lefevre Emerging Practitioner Fellowship from Ohio State University School of Architecture for 2003–2004. In 2005, the firm won the Young Architects Forum award from the Architectural League in New York.

Lola Sheppard is an Assistant Professor at the University of Waterloo School of Architecture. Mason White is an Assistant Professor at the University of Toronto Faculty of Architecture Landscape and Design.

Clearing

Toronto, ON

Trailing us like a shadow, we are only aware of our personal space when it has been compromised. Everyday our personal space is negotiated, wrested, if only temporarily, from the public realm and environment. Personal space is our first territorial line with our environment and others. This line expands and contracts in differing circumstances contingent upon our acceptance or willingness to engage with a given environment or body. How can this experience be physically simulated? Can we be made more aware of the impact of our personal space on others? Can people be empowered to create and manage the limits of the space they occupy?

Clearing is a commission for a room-sized interactive space that invites visitors to participate in the politics of personal space. Participants curate their own space though the manipulation of a dense fibrous field of black elastomeric cables using acrylic discs that gather the cables, like hair. The elastomeric cables can stretch up to 2 times their original length. Over 4000 cables are strung into loops and arranged with varying density across a grid of perforated metal sheets along a suspended ceiling and floor. The possible configurations are infinite and over its 4 month installation, it never ended the day the way it looked that morning.

Clearing highlights the role of an individual in a crowd, and the potential of crowd working collectively to create, sculpt and manage space relative to those around us.

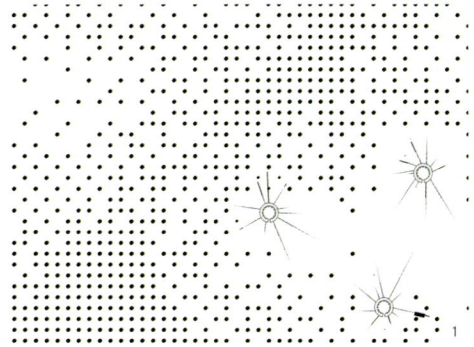

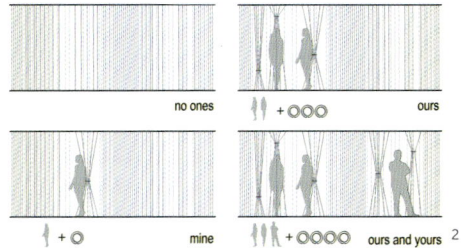

1

no ones   ours

+ 000

+ 0   mine   + 0000   ours and yours   2

1   Plan of cables field with various densities
2   Elevations showing occupation scenarios
3   Cables can stretch to more than twice their length
4   Clearing establishes a room within a room
5   Serrated acrylic disks gather cables to clear space

From Runways to Greenways
Reykjavik, Iceland

The project brief was to redevelop the terrain of a defunct air field in the city of Reykjavik, Iceland. The proposal seeks to use landscape and public space as a catalyst for urban development. It identifies exterior space as equally charged with activity, use and event, as built or interior spaces within the city.

Zones of the proposal are designated as "no-build" by converting the airport's former runways into "greenways." The greenways establish three primary axes of the site, each of which takes a quality of the city as a primary trait including ecology, recreation, and production.

The north-south runway is converted to primarily ecological and civic uses. A dot-matrix of micro-ecologies of varying uses and materials, including wetlands and hills, extends along this wide public greenway. The east-west greenway is a landscape of production, organized as a sustainable system of intake and yield for water, energy (geothermal), and food. It is designed as a bar code of interdependent production zones of varying densities, including aquaculture, sea water greenhouses producing fruit, vegetables and flowers, allotment gardens, markets, tree farming, and, below grade, server farms. The third greenway, oriented northeast-southwest, establishes a recreation corridor for four new neighbourhoods. Subdivided by roads, this greenway accommodates recreation 'rooms'; spaces for informal play, as well as soccer fields, track fields, tennis courts, as well as local schools and playgrounds.

The master plan divides the new Vatnsmyri district into four quadrants, corresponding to four proposed urban block typologies, differentiated in their programming, form, urban porosity, and extents of green or public space. Each block type varies in density and massing, but common amongst all the types is the intention of porosity. Blocks are either porous to the street, to sunlight, to terrace decks, or to foot traffic.

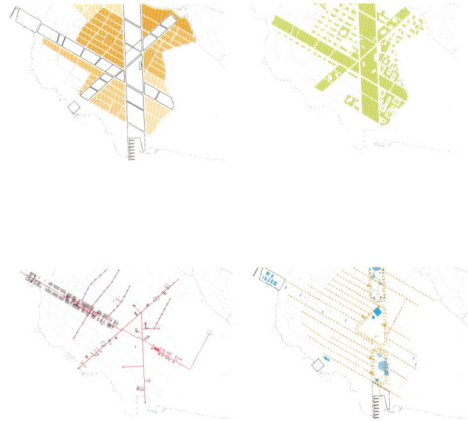

1

2

1   Urban diagrams: block types, open space, energy, water
2   Fragment of masterplan showing greenways and block types
3   Block and street typologies exhibiting degrees of porosity
4   Aerial of Vatnsmyri area showing the three greenways
5   View of public space along civic greenway

Lateral Office

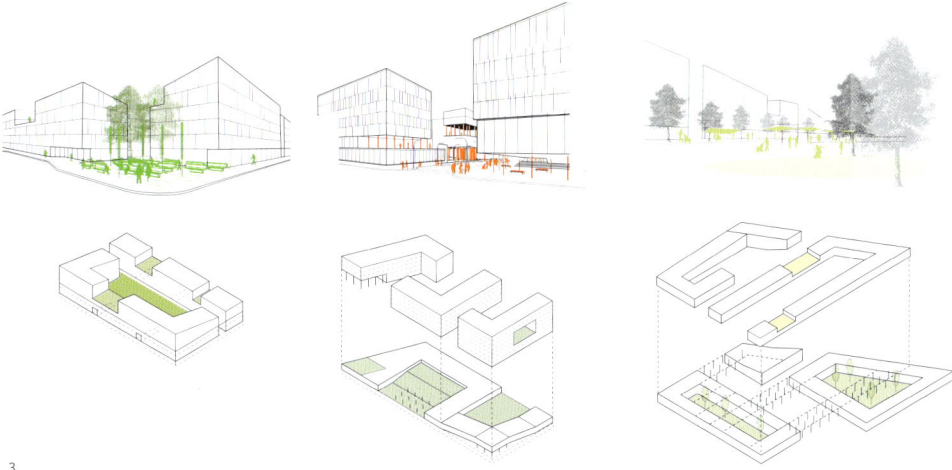

3

4

5

Marko Simcic Architect

Vancouver, British Columbia

Marko Simcic Architect is a small Vancouver-based practice, with two members, Marko Simcic, and Brian Broster. Projects undertaken by the firm are typically highly involved explorations, necessitating close interaction with our clients. Beginning without design preconceptions and evolving through an investigative, collaborative process, the work is generally informed by ongoing research and by the parallel art practice of the principal.

South Pender Island Retreat

South Pender Island, BC

This project is a retreat for a couple who live in Victoria, BC. The building, at about 2,500 square feet, consists of an open social space of kitchen, dining and living rooms, a study, a main bedroom and guest accommodation.

The property occupies the top of a sharp ridge, high above and inland from the surrounding ocean. It has a strong relationship to both a north and a south orientation, characterized by openness and distance, while the east and west sides remain treed and enclosing. This, together with steep grades falling to north and south, gives the site its fulcrum.

The project design began as a roof form, limiting and controlling while simultaneously emphasizing the specific qualities of the site and program. The roof orients and opens up to the north and south for light and view, while closing to the east and west for shade and privacy. The intermittent vertical drops in the roof provide structure and solar shading for summer afternoon sun angles. In the absence of trees to the south, the roof extends a large overhang to shade and protect against rain, wind, and summer sun, and captures reflected light from the ocean. In contrast, the shorter overhang on the north side provides exposure to the sky vault with daylight reflecting off roof-water collected on the north terrace. The height and angle variations of the ceiling surfaces provide the dynamic acoustic qualities required by the client for flute and piano playing.

Concrete slabs on grade, clad with black slate, provide passive solar thermal mass to augment the in-slab hydronic radiant heating. Each slab elevation was set in response to existing grade and bedrock elevations.

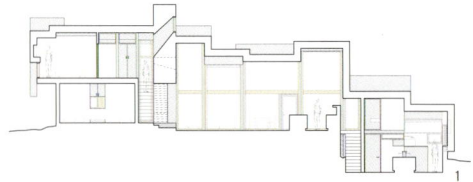

1

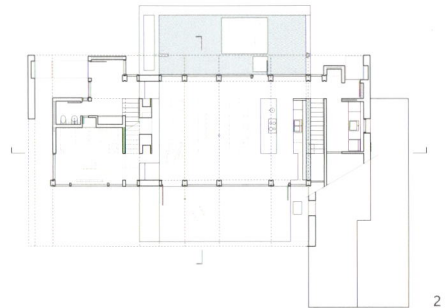

2

3

1 Section (view north)
2 Main floor plan (north up)
3 View from living room into study/den (view west)
4 View from southeast
5 Kitchen/dining room (view south)

Marko Simcic Architect

4

5

Metchosin House
Metchosin, BC

This residence for a retired couple and their extended family is located on a 67-acre oceanfront farm near Victoria, BC. The house is sited near the ocean, away from open agricultural lands and strong prevailing winds, in a draw (ravine) surrounded and shaded by mature Garry oaks. Concern for the trees' ecosystem drove the planning for the site. The critical root zones and branches of the grove were mapped and the winter groundwater flow pattern tracked. To preserve the trees, the house is sited where it would not cause damage to their roots or disturb their water supply–the two main reasons that Garry oaks have gone into serious decline in the region.

The design process traced the site explorations, the paths walked back and forth towards the edge of the ocean, and back up the draw through various open and enclosed spaces. The line that results is a conceptually clear, albeit very idiosyncratic ribbon of program that moves, folds, and shifts, negotiating the demands of the site and the building's spatial requirements. This creates a complex series of relationships, the most interesting of which engage the gap between the two long arms of program. This liminal space is defined by the hydrothermal system's flowing, the spent ocean water in the reflecting pool, and the ghosted images of the oak cladding from the outer boundary walls. Unlike the associative resonances of this spatial lacuna, the outer walls address the surrounding landscape directly. Garry oak ecosystems in the region are disappearing, threatened by development. This project, supported by an extensive research phase, takes on the responsibility of understanding and working with the ecology of the grove. Metchosin House is a demonstration of how architectural engagement can connect with the landscape in ways that heighten awareness of ecological challenges.

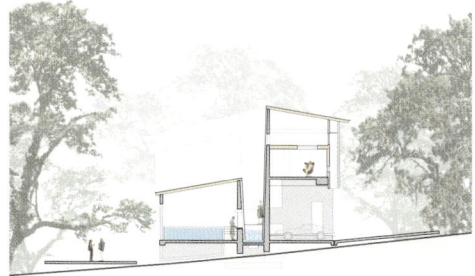

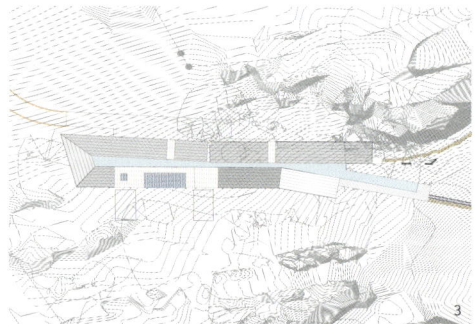

1   Cross section through ensuite/living room (view east)
2   Cross section through pool terrace/upper guest bedroom (view west)
3   Partial site plan (north up)
4   Reflecting pool (view northwest)
5   End of reflecting pool toward living room/bedroom (view west)
6   Reflecting pool from bridge/link (view east)
7   Living room with dining room/upper deck beyond (view southwest)

Marko Simcic Architect

5

6

7

mcfarlane | green | biggar ARCHITECTURE + DESIGN

North Vancouver, British Columbia

mcfarlane green biggar ARCHITECTURE + DESIGN (mgb) is a multidisciplinary architecture and design firm based in North Vancouver, BC. The firm has realized a wide range of residential, public, academic, and commercial commissions, from retail and restaurant designs to large-scale condominiums, public institutions and transportation projects.

It has always been the mandate of mgb to balance the large with the small, the local and national with the international. This philosophy of creative diversity leaves room for bold ideas, new thinking, and fresh perspectives.

The firm has won a number of awards including four Lieutenant Governor's Awards, an IDIBC Gold Award of Excellence, an international Wood Design Award and two British Columbia Wood Design Awards.

mgb strives to be a leader in the architecture and design industry through innovative uses of wood technology, based on sustainable principles. Currently, the firm is developing ideas for ultra-low-energy design under the Passivhaus principles with the ambition to reduce its projects' energy use to five percent of that used in conventional construction.

Prince George Airport
Prince George, BC

mcfarlane | green | biggar (mgb) was commissioned to design three phases of the Prince George Airport expansion and renovation. The mgb team has completed two of these phases to modernize and update the aging existing terminal.

Phase One added a new passenger hold room, screening systems, outbound baggage processing, and new airline offices. Phase Two further expanded the terminal with the addition of new international and domestic arrivals areas, and an international passenger customs processing facility. Work on the design of Phase Three is continuing, including renovations to the passenger check-in area and a new restaurant.

The design modernizes the 1970's terminal using a new structure of exposed heavy timber, concrete, and steel, with a focus on craft and elegance in the structural and envelope detailing. Durability, sustainability, and cost were all factored into the decision to develop a simple, natural palette for the building.

Arriving passengers are greeted with a sky-lit central atrium that serves as the primary circulation area, linking departing and arriving passengers. The dense structure is layered with a fir sunscreen and a steel and engineered-wood structure. A dynamic play of light and shadow transforms the space throughout the day. The Prince George community has embraced the building for its modern, materially expressive aesthetic. The community sees the airport redevelopment and the terminal's design as a catalyst for future growth and a strong symbolic gateway for commerce, industry, and tourism.

1   Passenger holdroom
2   Atrium glazing
3   View from landside
4   View from airside

3

4

Obakki
Vancouver, BC

Vancouver's flagship Obakki store promotes Canadian fashion designers' work with seasonal men's and women's lines. The client's requirement was a store design that supported the simple modern and evolving aesthetic of the brand's fashion, and offered a flexible environment for showcasing clothes, jewellery and accessories.

mcfarlane | green | biggar (mgb) was commissioned for the project in the late fall of 2006, with a very short schedule, to open for the Christmas-season rush.

mgb introduced a few simple design changes to the store in an effort to complement the elegant, minimalist aesthetic of the existing shell space. In collaboration with renowned Vancouver woodworker Brent Comber, the firm developed a signature piece for the store: a long wood counter by Comber, which mgb intersected with white solid surface folds for jewellery, a tea bar, point of sale, and storage.

In addition, mgb architects developed and built three custom light fixtures, using translucent acrylic suspended below simple box housings for hidden, inexpensive lighting.

The main display of clothing is handled with a "zero edge" soft-framed suspended white ceiling. The ceiling floats like a thin piece of paper and has custom stainless-steel clothes rods and hangers.

The red brick wall can be softened or neutralized by changing the configuration of fabric hung on a pair of concealed tracks running the length of the store. Two circular change rooms also incorporate floor-to-ceiling fabric curtains instead of fixed walls. The effect is a spacious openness when the change rooms are not in use, and a soft fabric counterpoint to the strong clean lines of the interior when the curtains are closed.

1   Jewellery display
2   Wood counter
3   View from entry
4   Fitting rooms

_naturehumaine [architecture+design]

Montréal, Québec

_naturehumaine is a Montréal architecture studio founded in 2003 by Stéphane Rasselet and Marc-André Plasse. The firm's work seeks to position architecture as a significant force in the evolution of contemporary ideas and lifestyles. They see architecture not as a simple design gesture but as a skilful response to symbolic, economic, sociological, and environmental issues. The premise of their design process is that each project has its own specific quality and context; the objective is to realize the potential of the site and create environments that are inspiring, dynamic, and unique.

Their wide range of work demonstrates their desire to explore the creative potentials of each project. Their work includes urban and rural residences, commercial and retail projects, restaurants, a municipal garage, and religious buildings. Since 2003 they have been involved in an ongoing project to rethink and renovate branches of a funeral home, researching ways to reinvent the image and tradition of the funeral in contemporary society. The firm has been on the short list of finalists in two major competitions in Québec: the design of a new Cistercian monastery, in 2004, and the design of a theatre in Dolbeau-Mistassini in 2006. Their residential projects have been featured in several Montréal newspapers over the past year. In 2007 the firm won a "prix de la relève" INTERIEUR FERDIE and also a Grand Prix Créativité Montréal for the design of Café Quattro D.

Quattro D
Montréal, QC

Located on St-Denis Street in Montréal, Quattro D presents a new concept for fast-food dining, halfway between a convenience store and a café. Healthy, quick, and inexpensive meals are offered to customers, to be eaten in the café or taken out, lunch-box style, to eat at work or home. The design challenge was to create a strong identity for the interior, conveying a double message of urbanity combined with the appeal and image of lovingly prepared homemade food.

The starting image was that of an urban picnic: a gigantic white tablecloth is lifted up, wrapping the ceiling and upper walls to meet the refrigerators. Derived from traditional Italian embroidery, the tablecloth pattern was hand-painted in the style of large-scale urban graffiti. Under this canopy, a central counter mounted on trestles zigzags through the space. On both sides, refrigerated cases offer colourful displays of tempting foods. In continuity with the concrete surface of the sidewalks, the floor is paved with large sheets of smooth fibrocement.

Informal and intimate, Quattro D is conceived of as the local store, to be visited on a daily basis.

1

2

3

1   Ceiling graphic detail
2   View from the service zone
3   Playful facade banner
4   Main space
5   View towards entrance
6   Street counter

_naturehumaine [architecture+design]

Résidence Garnier

Montréal, QC

Located in the heart of the Plateau Mont-Royal neighbourhood, the project involves the renovation of an old 1920s triplex to create a new home for a young couple and their two children.

The existing building had been neglected for years and was in need of a thorough and vigorous intervention. First, all partitions were removed from the two upper storeys. A central vertical volume containing stairs, bathrooms, and closets was inserted, becoming the focal point around which all the rooms are arranged. Covered with natural strawboard, this functional volume provides a unifying visual background for every space in the house.

Along the perimeter walls, the old wooden structure of the triplex is exposed at intervals, as an archaeological artifact revealing the constitutive framework of the house. The existing structure connects seamlessly with the new oiled ipe wood floor, creating a sense of continuity between past and present.

The entrance door and cloakroom are discreetly hidden behind a pivoting panel. Covered with dark blue cork and two mirrors, this panel becomes a playful display surface for the children.

Designed around the existing openings, the new street façade consists of a play of alternating masonry panels. A cantilevered canopy marks the entrance while a boxed-in garden animates the interface between the house and the street.

The use of raw and natural materials infuses the house with a sense of serenity and authenticity. Its human scale and carefully distributed spaces offer a welcoming atmosphere for this contemporary urban dwelling.

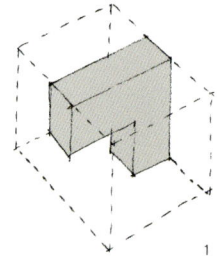

1   Diagram showing the inserted central volume
2   View of the reading room, second floor
3   Kitchen, ground floor
4   Living room with pivoting panel, ground floor
5   Street facade with boxed-in garden
6   Rear facade
7   Central stair with old wooden structure and skylight

_naturehumaine [architecture+design]

NIPpaysage

Montréal, Québec

Seeking a renewed vision of landscape architecture,
the design team at NIPpaysage looks to each
project's individual cultural and social implications
for inspiration. The objective is to reveal the true
character of the site and the environment, and to
create a unique and meaningful spatial composition.
The narrative character of the firm's work combines
conceptual and functional issues, which are essential
ingredients in the creation of successful landscape
design. NIPpaysage is particularly fascinated by the
everyday, common spaces that are often forgotten
or ignored in traditional definitions of landscape.
These spaces are perceived as opportunities for
the creation of new and stimulating landscape
experiences. NIPpaysage's work involves the
planning and design of landscape projects, ranging
from small installation projects to large master-
planning efforts. The work stands apart for its
optimism, using a colourful and inventive approach.

NIPpaysage is currently working on the Gatineau
Sports Centre, which will be home to the 2010
Québec Games finals, and completing work on the
restoration of the Cross on Mount Royal. The firm is
also involved with an ongoing study of Lafontaine
Park and is wrapping up design for the Canada
pavilion for the 2010 Shanghai world exposition.

Beaten Track

Québec City, QC

The object of the Ephemeral Gardens competition was to create designs to be included in the 2008 celebration of the four-hundredth anniversary of the founding of Québec City. Far from being simply the contemplative experience of a classic garden, the Ephemeral Gardens project invited entrants to discover, experience, and participate in an artistic event that would bring together creators from the many different disciplines and origins that have influenced our culture. NIPpaysage's *Beaten Track* is one of twelve gardens proposed by architects, landscape architects, and visual artists, each bringing an individual perspective to the 400th anniversary year.

Playing with variations on the log as a garden component, *Beaten Track* explores a rustic construction material par excellence, using motifs derived from good old-fashioned woodcutting; the log is multiplied to fill an entire garden. From the living tree to the log, a sculpted space comes into being —a composition both playful and sophisticated. The assembly is a hybrid space, half forest and half city. In the end, the garden invites us to step off the beaten path for an experience of open space with its myriad possible pathways.

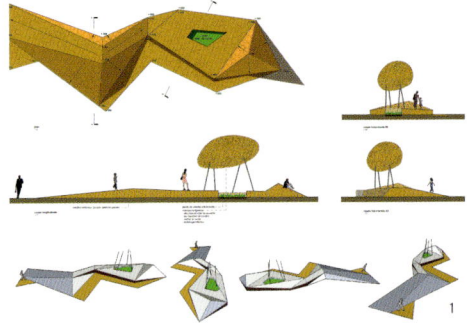

1 Drawings showing project's topographic complexity
2 Playful atmosphere generated by the origami-like folding of surfaces
3 Detail of edges revealing side of logs
4 Atmospheric view generated during design process
5 Night view of installation

4

5

Point Pleasant Park

Halifax, NS

In the fall of 2003, Hurricane Juan made landfall in Point Pleasant Park, a wooded urban oasis in Halifax, NS. Two-thirds of the 185-acre forest was destroyed, resetting the ecological clock of the park overnight. Looking for help with the reconstruction process, the city held an international design competition to find a team of landscape architects to redesign Point Pleasant. In 2005, NIPpaysage and Ekistics, co-winners of the competition, were selected to prepare a comprehensive one-hundred-year plan.

The plan needed to find a way to balance and reconcile conflicts between ecological and cultural values, and to develop a system of visual resource management for the park. To do this, the team found practical ways to build on theoretical research from a variety of different fields, drawing on science, history, and their own artistic vision to create a comprehensive adaptive-management plan for the forest, shoreline, and cultural remnants in the park.

The resulting Comprehensive Plan for Point Pleasant Park is based on cutting-edge applied landscape research, including cultural resource management, forest ecology for hurricane-prone landscapes, forest aesthetics, shoreline management (taking into consideration the potential for rising sea levels over the next century), visual resource management, and environmental design. An important goal of the plan was that it be understandable to the community and able to be implemented by the municipality.

The first major phase of the comprehensive plan will be implemented over the next five years. The plan has become a model for other Halifax Regional Municipality parks and other urban nature parks around the world.

1   Sections showing phased forest regeneration
2   Great ocean amphitheatre – view to Halifax harbour and ribbon forest
3   Site analysis diagrams
4   View of proposed development at Cambridge Road Gateway
5   View of proposed shoreline restoration public amenities

NIPpaysage

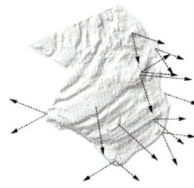

Pathways

Witness Groves
(Needle-leaved dominant)

Topography

Views

South Facing Slopes
(Broad-leaved dominant)

3

4

5

North Design Office

Toronto, Ontario

North Design Office is a landscape architecture, urbanism, and design firm based in Toronto. The firm was founded by partners Pete and Alissa North in 2005. Before establishing North Design Office, Pete worked at the offices of Martha Schwartz and Janet Rosenberg and Associates, and Alissa at Hargreaves Associates and Urban Strategies. The Norths both graduated from the Bachelor of Landscape Architecture Program at the University of Toronto and from the Master of Landscape Architecture Program at Harvard University. In addition to their work at North Design Office, they are also both assistant professors in the Faculty of Architecture, Landscape, and Design at the University of Toronto.

At North Design Office, research and theory inform a process-based approach to complex urban environmental issues. Projects range in scale from site-specific art installations to architecture and urban design, with an emphasis on landscape architecture. A unique design strategy is created for each project, founded on an intensive exploration of site, context, and program as the mechanism for transformation. The office is committed to the idea that well-designed urban environments and open spaces create vibrant ecologies, communities, and cities.

The Verdant Walk

Cleveland, Ohio, USA

Once a powerhouse of industry, Cleveland, Ohio, is moving out of a period of decline and into a new era of sustainable development, based on alternative sources of energy and the thoughtful evolution of urban design. The Verdant Walk, both a landscape and public art installation for Mall B in downtown Cleveland, is an imaginative response to the city's industrial heritage and its new green agenda. The sculpted aluminum frames offer a reminder of the community's long history of manufacturing and industry, and their organic podlike shapes capture a sense of evolution toward a smarter, more sustainable future. When the forms are covered with translucent green fabric, integrated solar panels illuminate the forms from within using LED lights. Changing with the weather and the season, the Verdant Walk aspires to reconnect people to the natural rhythms and energies of their environment. In spring and summer, the installation responds to its environment with textures, translucency, shade, the rustling of tall native grasses, and glowing solar-powered lighting. In the fall and winter months, the green fabric covers are removed from the forms like leaves falling from a tree, allowing the bare, pure metal frames to cast long winter shadows. Alluding to moving water and responding to wind and weather, linear plantings of tall grasses are interspersed with spaces of the open green lawn of Mall B. Made up of a diverse mixture of native Ohio grasses, they celebrate the inseparability of Cleveland from its natural landscape, the Cuyahoga River, and its waterfront location on Lake Erie.

Gathering like a herd of friendly beasts, and glowing with welcome, the forms of the Verdant Walk invite visitors to join them as they lead the way to a green future.

1

2

3

1   Winter perspective of installation
2   Standing form with other herd members
3   Forms within native grasses
4   Illuminated forms
5   Integrated solar film collects energy for evening illumination
6   A visitor examines an illuminated form

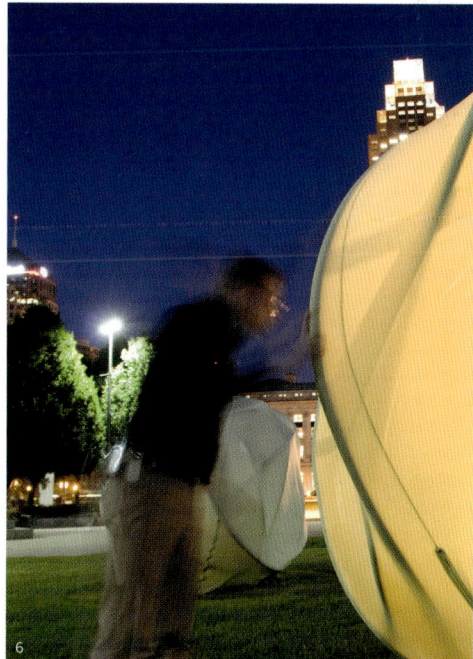

Paul Raff Studio

Toronto, Ontario

Paul Raff is an architect and artist who began his
creative practice in 1993 and incorporated as
an architecture firm in 2003. His studio employs
experts in architecture, development strategy,
landscape and interior design. Based in Toronto,
the firm works locally and internationally,
with projects currently being developed in
North America, South America, and Asia.

The firm's collaborative environment is dedicated to
creative production of the highest calibre. The goal
is to create projects in which art and architecture
combine to enhance the client's life. Paul Raff
Studio's experience ranges widely in scale and scope,
including master-planning, urban design, private
residences and gardens, cultural and commercial
buildings, video installations, and public art work.

Cascade House

Toronto, ON

Cascade House is perched on a gently sloping site in Toronto, Ontario. In response to the clients' love of contemporary art and their desire for natural light, the design's sculptural forms are both aesthetic and functional, harnessing sunlight to augment interior comfort. In the living room, a 13-foot-high screen of stacked sheets of jagged-cut glass maximizes sunlight while also providing privacy from the street. Reminiscent of a waterfall, it draws connections to the adjacent pool and imparts texture and movement into the room. The screen is made of 475 glass panels stacked vertically in a crenellated pattern; the glass creates light, shadows, and colours that change atmosphere and emotional effect kaleidoscopically through the course of the day.

A complement to the translucent screen is a freestanding, monolithic wall of slate that acts as a central spine. It rises from the lower level of the house to the top floor, creating a unified visual connection. It is also a passive-solar heat sink: set behind south-facing glass, it absorbs the sun's energy during cold winter days, and slowly disperses its heat overnight. Framing the feature staircase, it rises from the lower level of the house to the top floor. Random apertures provide display spaces for art works or niches for children to play in; the cut-outs also dapple the spaces beyond with light. The pattern of slate is designed with varying rough and polished surfaces to further play with the reflection and absorption of light.

Simple yet materially rich, Cascade House evokes a casual yet sophisticated aesthetic, with every detail functioning as part of the overall artistic vision.

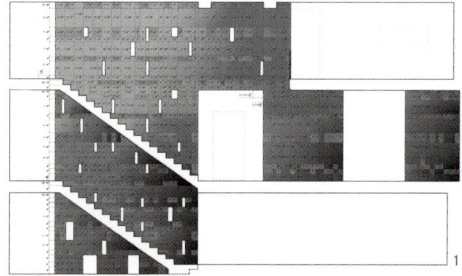

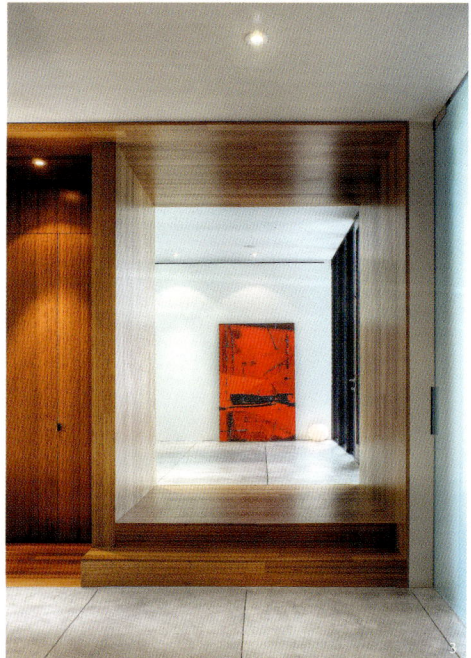

1   Elevation drawing of the slate wall
2   View of living room with stacked glass screen beyond
3   Stained bamboo panelling connects the entrance to the living room
4   Dusk view across the pool
5   View of sculptural staircase next to the slate wall
6   Slate wall provides cubbyholes and a giant
    chalkboard in children's playroom

RVTR

Toronto, Ontario

RVTR is concerned with the role and agency of design of the built environment in an era of rapid climate change, faltering energy supplies, tightening global networks and radical new technologies that fundamentally change the very meaning of space, time, and the human body. RVTR's partners, Kathy Velikov, Geoffrey Thün, Colin Ripley and Paul Raff are engaged in academic work in parallel with professional endeavours, and the firm's mandate is to pursue an agenda of interdisciplinary opportunities. Projects evolve through co-production and collaboration with the academic sphere, industry, and government agencies. This alternative model of practice is predicated on the need for freedom to engage critical issues and operate as creative problem seekers, rather than the more conventional problem solvers of standard service-based architectural practices.

In 2008, RVTR received a Young Architects Forum Award from the Architectural League of New York. In 2008 their work was exhibited in New York City and at the Design at Riverside Gallery in Cambridge.

Post Carbon Highway

Ontario| Great Lakes Megaregion

The Post-Carbon Highway is a regional urban infrastructure design/research project that explores the possible consequences of the depletion of carbon-based fuels. Shortages of such fuels could precipitate the demise of the automotive and transport industries and a collapse of global trade networks. Alternatively, the threat of such a worldwide oil crash could become the urgent impetus for change, leading to the creation of new fuels and more efficiently interconnected regional urbanities and infrastructures.

The proposal focuses its speculative visualization of a post-carbon world on southern Ontario's Highway 401, North America's most densely travelled highway, a key conduit for international trade, and a work-home connector for 40 percent of the Canadian population. Given current systems and supply, the highway's future would seem to be one of imminent congestion and failure.

The RVTR project, based on a wide range of current research, presents a different picture, sizing up the potential value of a single, intensive, highly linear system. The cross-sectional densification of the line accommodates not only increased traffic, but also multiple modes of traffic types, velocities, and energy sources in a highly mobile post-carbon future. The matrix of parallel, cooperative transit routes will maximize temporal efficiency, safety, and accessibility, with high-speed rail, dedicated freight and vehicle lanes configured in a "thick" system that effectively increases the bandwidth of the line by stacking and separating transport types. As a result, the line will become the robust infrastructural backbone of a proximate urbanism. Refueling systems will be provided at every service point, along with freight distribution facilities, temporary accommodations, and recreational opportunities. These multimodal transfer interchanges will become the key urban node along the highway, as post-carbon-era travellers interface with a new multicentred type of urban region.

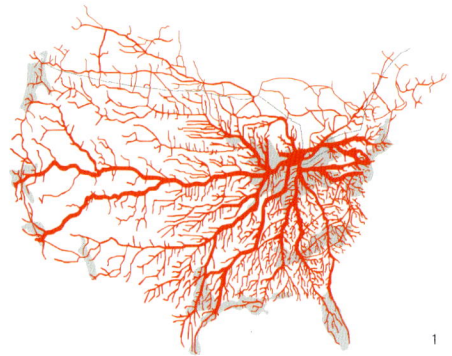

1

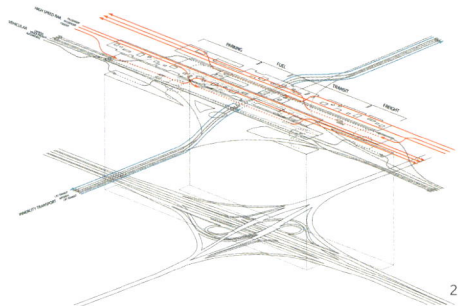

2

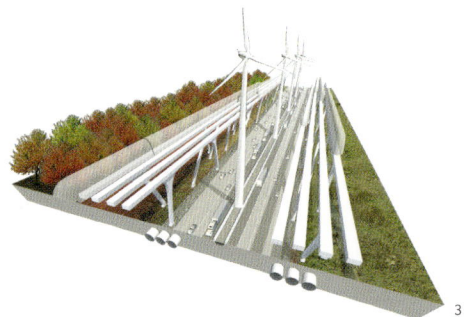

3

1   Transnational freight flows and emerging North American megaregions
2   Multimodal transfer interchange: flows and uses
3   Post-Carbon Highway: parallel cooperative networks
4   Multimodal transfer interchange: bird's-eye view
5   Multimodal transfer interchange: freight section

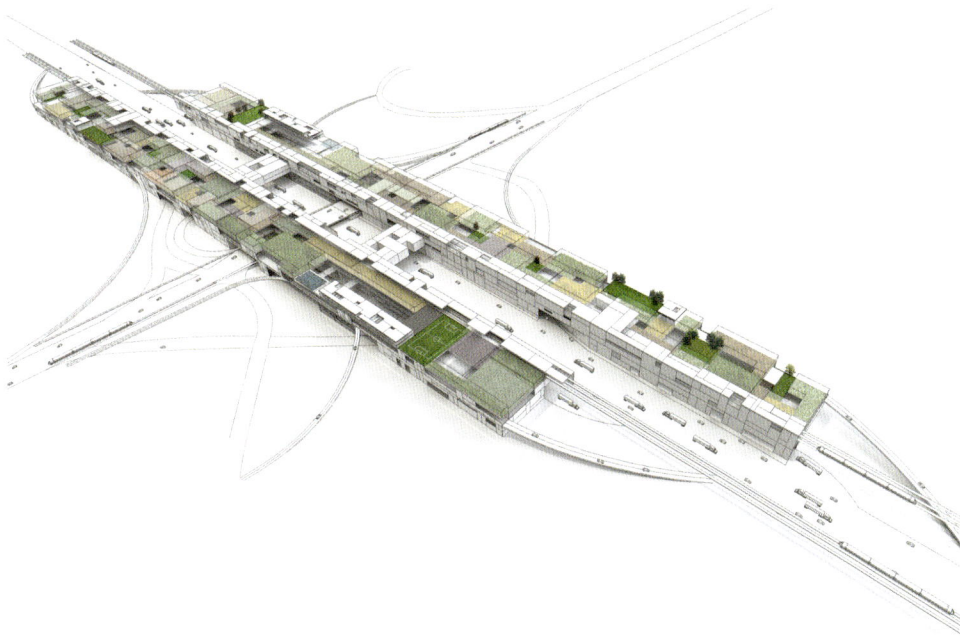

4

5

Latitude Housing System

Cherepovets, Russia

The Latitude housing system, which received an Honorable Mention in the 2008 Living Steel Extreme Housing Competition, is a proposal for sustainable housing that operates as an agent in transforming the housing industry by engaging component-based manufacturing processes, making high-performance sustainable housing available to the average homeowner and stimulating new industries and marketable products. Latitude proposes a system of prefabricated, highly engineered, lightweight steel modular units that perform quadruple duty as an energy-efficient building envelope, integrated structural system, space defining elements, and infrastructural chassis for building services such as power, data, water, waste, and HVAC (heating, ventilation and air conditioning). The system allows for a wide variety of configurations and for ready adaptation to respond to future needs.

Latitude makes use of high-performance glazing systems developed by the firm in partnership with researchers at the University of Waterloo and glazing industry partners, (for an entry to the Solar Decathlon 2009 competition). The team has developed a glazing system that can be a net energy producer at high latitudes with relatively scarce solar resources. When paired with active shading systems, this development radically changes the way we think about northern housing and available light. The house no longer needs be a highly internalized domain with minimal openings, but can instead be opened up to the exterior landscape, offering highly energy-efficient housing that is at the same time filled with natural light and intimately connected to the outdoors.

The houses are designed to be aggregated into sustainable communities that minimize land use and capitalize on the potential of cooperative energy-producing systems, such as solar thermal, wind, and waste processing, as well as local independent food production.

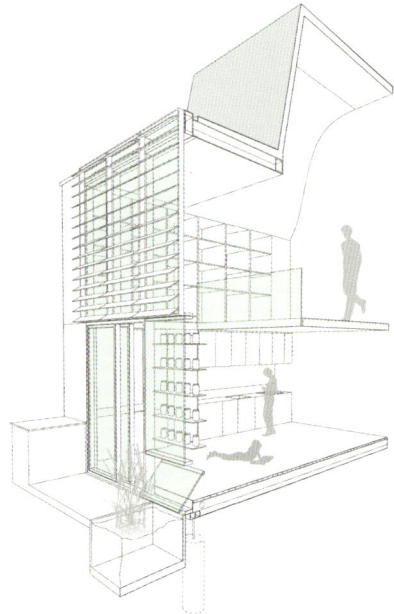

1

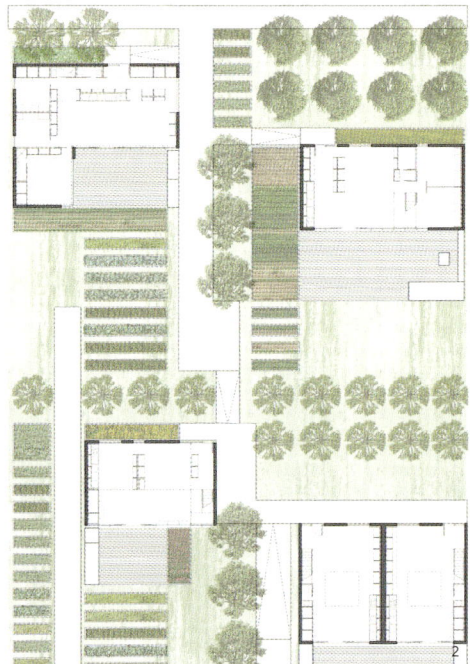

2

1   Section cutaway of layered technologies and assemblies
2   Partial site plan of Latitude housing aggregation
3   Latitude green-house type, winter view
4   Latitude courtyard-house type, interior view
5   Latitude loft-house type with productive landscape

spmb
Winnipeg, Manitoba

spmb (São Paulo Manitoba) is a collaborative
art, architecture and design practice, created
in 1998 by Eduardo Aquino and Karen Shanski.
spmb questions traditional notions of artistic and
architectural practices in the public realm through
interdisciplinary strategies including research,
design, teaching, publishing, guerrilla action
(unapproved, adventurous intrusions in urban
spaces), and any other effective means to activate
public space. spmb searches for situations where
architecture presents itself as an ongoing process of
unfolding, and where scale, context, and materiality
are deployed broadly, and respond specifically to
each situation encountered. In its response, spmb is
committed to creating a new understanding of the
practice of art/architecture, an understanding that
is at the same time technologically adventurous,
politically critical, and socially responsible.
This hybrid collaboration seeks to subvert the
instrumental view of architecture and the narrow
categorization of art as an elusive discipline. Recent
site-responsive projects in the public domain
include: *Vous êtes ici* (Public Art Project for the
Maison de la culture Maisonneuve, Montréal, 2005);
Table of Contents (Public Art Project for Vimy Ridge
Park, Winnipeg, 2006), *Copan Projects*, presented
at Casa Vertigo (Technical University of Eindhoven,
the Netherlands, 2007), and *Plage* (Festival Jardins
Éphémères, Québec City, 2008). spmb was selected
to participate in the 2009 edition of the Jardins
de Métis / Reford Gardens International Garden
Festival in Métis, Québec. *Complex Order: Intrusions
in Public Space*, a book by spmb, was published
in 2009 by Plug In Editions (www.plugin.org).

Plage

Québec City, QC

*There is no such thing as an empty space or an empty time.
There is always something to see, something to hear. In fact,
try as we may to make a silence—we cannot.* John Cage

As a public space, the beach suggests new possibilities
for social conciliation. There, visitors with different
cultural backgrounds, ethnic roots and socioeconomic
class can share the same landscape in pleasant
harmony. The beach becomes an ideal urban social
equalizer—a hypersocial spatialized democracy. The
prairie, in contrast, is a space of introspection and
reflection. The vast horizon and the open skies invite
one to look into infinity and consider one's solitude.

To celebrate the four hundred years of Québec City, a
dialogue between landscapes (Plage-Prairie-Québec)
was proposed. The project is based on the prairie/
beach typology, which it explores through sound,
light, colour, and planting in a space reminiscent of
the fields and open spaces of the prairie, juxtaposed
with the enticement of the beach's culture of play and
soft landscape. *Plage* creates a counterpoint to the
typical garden experience. It is not a garden with an
emphasis on display, but rather a garden whose primary
purpose is experiential: a space for meeting, gathering,
observation, introspection, and above all, for encounters.

The garden created by spmb is an open field of
possibilities. The garden is an animated ambient, a
multisensorial field where the visitor is invited to engage
with the ground and sloping surfaces, the LED lighting,
flower circles, sun suckers, and fragrant lavender/
grass rows. *Plage* proposes not the simple transfer
of the prairie/beach typology to the urban space of
Québec City, but instead a garden concept in which the
strategy of inter-landscaping incorporates the minimal
geometry and specific qualities of these landscapes in
order to celebrate in Québec the encounter of cultures.

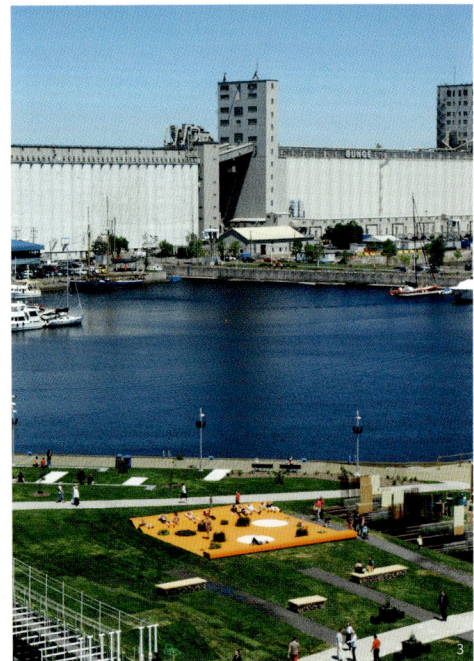

1   Section
2   General view in front of the Bunge grain elevators
3   In front of the Bunge grain elevators at the Bassin Louise in Québec City
4   Linear chaise longue with sound components around the headspace
5   General view

Table of Contents

Winnipeg, MB

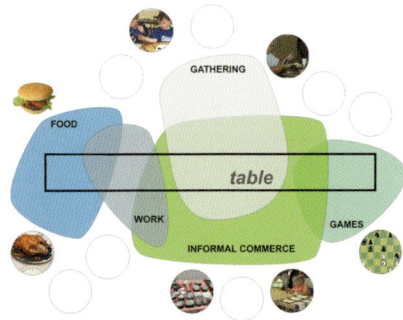

Being involved with the arts can have a lasting and transforming effect on many aspects of people's lives. This is true not just for individuals, but also for neighbourhoods, communities, regions and entire generations, whose sense of identity and purpose can be changed through art. Peter Hewitt, *Who will be transformed?*

Table of Contents was the theme of a national competition sponsored by the Public Art Program of the Winnipeg Arts Council. Inspired by the existing park tables at Vimy Ridge Memorial Park, spmb created a table with sculptural proportions programmed to accommodate multiple activities by diverse park users.

Through language, we establish relationships and build community. spmb invited the people of Wolseley to contribute words to be inscribed on the Table project. Each household was asked to provide a five-word phrase that represented a sentiment about the place: a desire, a dream, or the memory of an event that took place in the neighbourhood. With all the collected phrases, spmb composed a narrative, a story, a history of Wolseley—a landscape of language.

Monuments, including the ones in Vimy Ridge Park, commemorate heroic events of the past. The Canadians who fought at Vimy Ridge are remembered for their victory and their sacrifices for the freedom of generations to come. Perhaps now, after ninety-two years, we are at a threshold of change, where a new notion of celebration is being born to promote peace and communication amongst people. Public art challenges the traditional notion of the "historical monument" by reinventing public space, and unveiling new modes of celebration that place the public at the centre. *Table of Contents* addresses the notion of a living history: it records the words and memories of the people of the community, commemorating the moment as it is lived.

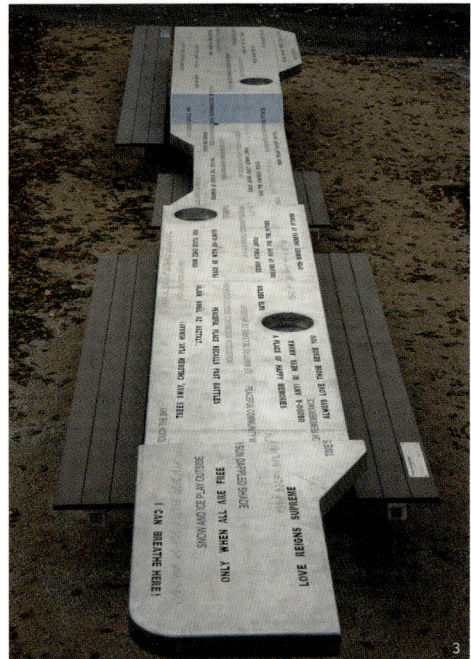

1   Diagram
2   Detail
3   A landscape of language
4   Hotdog roast
5   General view

Susan Fitzgerald Architecture

Halifax, Nova Scotia

Architecture frames our existence and conditions our lives. It also directs the allocation of collective resources. At a time when architecture is dominated by a culture of consumerism, temporary fashion and image, it is important to preserve memory, value, and meaning.

Susan Fitzgerald and her partner, Brainard Fitzgerald, design and build together. The locations are typically in-between spaces that due to scale, topography, or lack of services are undesirable to mainstream development. Working intimately with these sites and the process of construction, the architect and her partner experience the subtleties and possibilities of a place. Plans are drawn directly on the land to fully comprehend topography and massing. Staging is erected to assess outlook and scale. Constant visits to the site reveal weathering patterns, microclimates and the changing seasons and light.

The work explores specifics of site and place. However, it is the intimacy between design and construction that really shapes the work. It provides the ongoing dialogue that influences not only the construction, the type of projects pursued, and the detailing, but the very essence of the work.

26 Bridgeview Drive

Halifax, NS

The house explores the blending of site and
building. It is an architecture of emplacement
that blurs the boundary between building
and land, culture, and place.

The house is located on a steeply sloping, wooded
site with granite boulder outcrops, on the outskirts of
Halifax, Nova Scotia. The limited budget necessitated
a pragmatic design approach and a small footprint.
Early investigation on the site shaped the floor
plans to eliminate rock and tree removal and tie
the building into the bedrock. Composed of two
blocks that appear to have slid down the slope, the
house nestles into the land. Between the two forms
a bridge or threshold links the house to the street.
In section, windows separate the two forms, while a
stair braces the building and roots it to the ground.

To allow the site to be experienced at many levels, the
house was organized as a four-storey plan stepping from
the road to the forest floor, with every part of the plan
accessible. Outdoor gathering/play areas have been
created on the roof, among the treetops, on the deck
and bridge that extend from the main living space and
between the granite boulders littered on the forest floor.

The house is constructed from conventional 2x6
platform framing on a concrete foundation. Birch
cabinets, stairs, and doors quietly contrast with the
white gypsum walls, stainless steel counters, and
polished concrete floors. The exterior cladding is a
tight skin of eastern cedar shingles with woven corners.
The courses are sculpted to the land's changing
topography, and the overall design explores local
material traditions within a modern aesthetic.

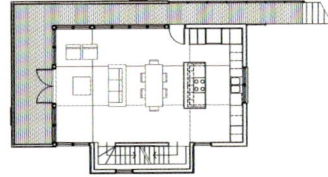

1

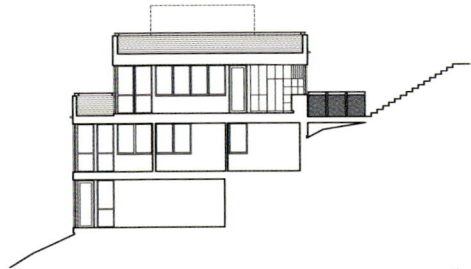

2

3

4

1   Level 3 (main and entry level) plan
2   Section through site and building
3   View from kitchen
4   View of house from below
5   View of house from road
6   South Corner
7   View of bedroom from doorway

Susan Fitzgerald Architecture

2061 Elm Street

Halifax, NS

This house explores personal and collective experiences of dwelling, of spaces and places stored in memory. It resonates with the site, the street, and the city. It is timeless yet modern, understanding its lineage while also addressing the future. This building embodies the form and history of the place. Like most of its neighbours, the house has cedar shingle cladding and shares the neighbourhood grammar of porches and window projections - it clearly fits, but it is also clearly different.

Located in a dense neighbourhood in the west end of Halifax, Nova Scotia, on a 25x100-foot lot, this 1,800-square-foot house was built on an existing 18 x24-foot foundation. Spread over four floors, it is the home of the architect, the builder, and their two children.

This project re-evaluates space and place. It is square-foot-frugal but spatially generous. Many elements within the design have multiple functions. Stair railings double as bookcases on the interior, and planters or benches on the exterior. The house and its neighbour share a driveway that, together with the shed/workshop, forms a sheltered courtyard for winter parking, a children's play area, outdoor workspace, and a flower garden.

At the heart of the plan is the kitchen table, simultaneously a place for preparing food, a dining table, a workspace, homework surface, and storage chest. The materials are simple and efficient and in the vocabulary of local construction. The natural cedar shingle skin provides an efficient and durable envelope for the harsh Nova Scotian climate. The polished concrete floors provide the thermal mass for the in-floor heating system.

Designed by the architect and built by her contractor husband, the house was created with a complete harmony of intent. This symbiotic relationship and ongoing dialogue improved design and details as construction materials, processes, and costs were continually assessed.

1   Level 2 (street level) plan
2   West and south elevation
3   View from bedroom looking west
4   View from kitchen looking west
5   View of shed and house from east
6   West (street) elevation
7   View of stair and bookcase railings

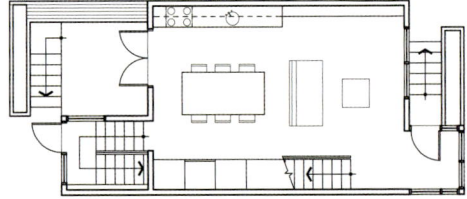

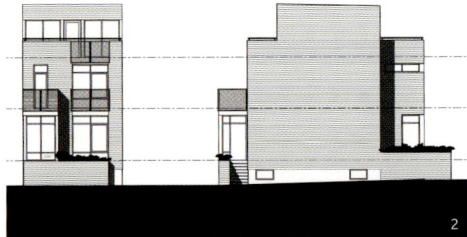

Susan Fitzgerald Architecture

The Acre Collective

Saint John, New Brunswick

The idea for the Acre Collective started on a rooftop in Brooklyn, New York, where a group of artists, writers, thinkers and designers realized that—working together—they could contribute more significantly than any one of them working alone. Conceived as a fresh and flexible way to tackle projects and ideas, the collective brings together the right team for the right project. Founders and team corrallers are Stephen Kopp and Monica Adair, master's of architecture graduates from the architecture and design program at the University of Toronto. They are currently based in the Maritimes.

The collective has been involved in projects that emphasize craftsmanship, functionality, local tradition, and artistic expression. At the core of the group's philosophy is an understanding of the unique opportunity that creative collaboration offers for the exploration of new ideas and the achievement of new outcomes. Projects realized collectively have the potential for a larger impact both socially and sustainably.

The core Acre team is joined by the architect, writer, and historian John Leroux, for the design of a summer house in St. Andrews scheduled for construction in late 2009.

hapito

Saint John, NB

Set within a prominent historic building in Saint John, NB, the "happinez" wine bar is home to a sidewalk patio, nicknamed "hapito" as a fusion of the two words.

Limited to just 5 feet deep by 25 feet long, this was a small project and space was at a premium. The simple linear layout is enclosed by an arrangement of interlocking wood members. Three rising floor decks below a continuous, level bar surface allow for multiple seating and standing combinations for patrons as the patio accommodates the sloped topography.

The motif of closely spaced vertical wood members makes for an elegant convergence of the street's steep sidewalk with the historical building's horizontal facade. The rhythmic patterning of solid surfaces and open spaces allows for interplay between privacy and transparency. A screened image of tall grasses injects nature into the urban landscape.

The principal wood used was local tamarack, selected as much for its natural resistance to rot and salt air as for its striking grain and texture. Careful consideration of its durability and inherent beauty led to the creation of inspired details. A cantilevered bench and bar reveals the strength of the solid wood, while the distinctive curvaceous pattern of the tamarack's end grain is featured along the edge of the cantilevered bar. The dominant motifs are carried through to custom-made wooden patio furniture. As a seasonal program, hapito was designed with modular joinery detailing that allows it to be taken apart for winter storage in three pieces.

1

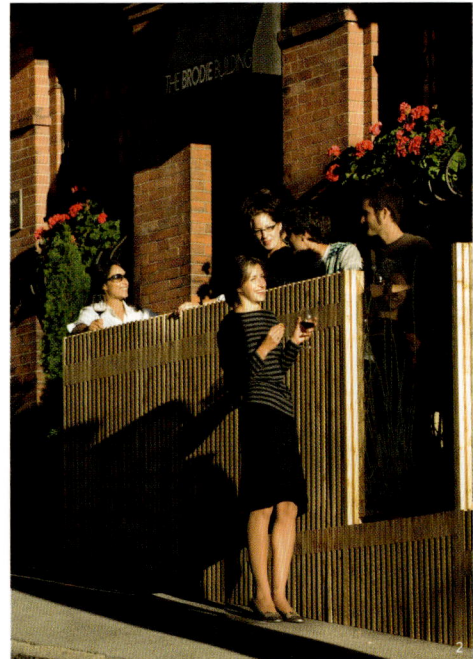

2

1   Street elevation
2   Interaction with pedestrians on sidewalk
3   View from first landing
4   hapito from above

The Acre Collective

Urban Republic arts society / ph5 architecture inc.

Vancouver, British Columbia

Vancouver's Urban Republic arts society and ph5 architecture inc. were officially founded in 2008 by Henning Knoetzele and Peeroj Thakre. Ph5 architecture inc. provides architectural services to clients for residential, commercial, and institutional projects. Urban Republic is a registered non-profit composed of artists, writers, and architects. The organization is a vehicle to research, develop, and implement speculative projects that use the tools of art and design to cultivate a sense of place and opportunities for social engagement. The process operates at the intersection of art, architecture, and urbanism. Urban Republic collaborates with artists, designers, communities and institutions to transform seemingly familiar and generic landscapes into vibrant public places.

In 2005, Urban Republic's founding members were the driving force behind FrontierSpace, an international design competition that transformed an alley into a viable public space, with a dramatic installation of oversized illuminated balloons.

In 2007, they designed and built the audio-video installation Garden Party, and in 2008 captured local and national media acclaim for the Gastown Drive-In.

Urban Republic is now at work on Gastown Drive-In: The Sequel, and a proposal for a suburban waterfront area in the Lower Mainland.

The Gastown Drive-in
Vancouver, BC

In September 2008, Urban Republic transformed the roof level of the EasyPark parkade in downtown Vancouver into a drive-in for both car-equipped and pedestrian audiences for a celebration of BC film. The theme of the film series was "Vancouver Stars as Itself." Selected shorts and feature films, shot wholly or in part within the Metro Vancouver area, showcased the talents of BC filmmakers. Admission to the screenings was free and accessible to all. After each screening, audience members were invited to meet the filmmakers.

The strength of the project lay in the thoughtful adaptation of roof topography, careful observation of the cycle for parking demand, and the fit of the proposed programming with the social and cultural context.

As with many downtown parking garages, the city-owned Gastown car park is full during the day and nearly empty at night. This diurnal cycle offered the possibility of a temporary expansion of the public realm at night in a neighbourhood with a shortage of outdoor public spaces.

The existing use and topography of the roof supported the drive-in proposal. The screen was mounted on the higher roof of an adjacent building, to achieve clear sight lines and reduce the height and corresponding loads of the temporary structure. The seating area sloped downward for optimal viewing from each area. The screen was designed so that the projected image appears to float in the skyline of the city.

Vancouver is the third-largest film production centre in North America, albeit usually as Hollywood's stand-in for another city. The film programming for the Gastown Drive-In became an opportunity to explore Vancouver's identity through the eyes of its filmmakers. The provocative venue became an enticement to draw in broad new audiences for BC film.

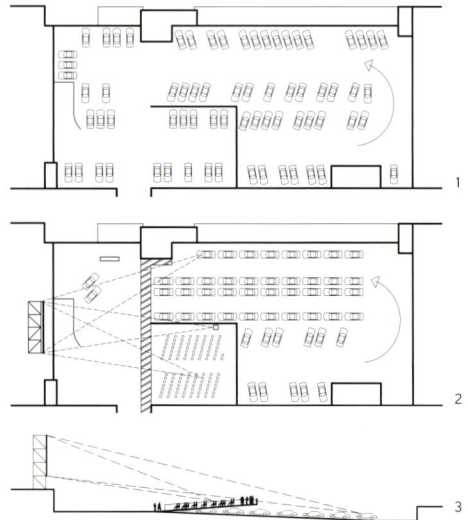

1   Conventional daytime parking/ floor plan
2   Event night parking / floor plan
3   Section
4   Event image showing empty levels of parking below
5   Event image, car area
6   Event image, seating area

Urban Republic arts society / ph5 architecture inc.

5

6

Project Credits

5468796 Architecture Inc.

210-63 Albert Street
Winnipeg, Manitoba R3B 1G4
T 204 480 8421
F 204 480 8876
www.5468796.ca
info@5468796.ca

youCUBE
Design team: Sharon Ackerman, Mandy Aldcorn,
Ken Borton, Aynslee Hurdal, Johanna Hurme,
Cristina Ionescu, Grant LaBossiere, Colin
Neufeld, Sasa Radulovic, Shannon Wiebe
Location: Winnipeg, Manitoba
Area: 18,500 s.f. (18 units)
Completion: 2010 (phase 1)
Construction: Artisan Homes
Structural: Hanuschak Consultants Inc.
Civil: MEC Consulting
Renderings: 5468796 Architecture Inc.

BGBX
Design team: Sharon Ackerman, Mandy Aldcorn,
Ken Borton, Aynslee Hurdal, Johanna Hurme,
Cristina Ionescu, Grant LaBossiere, Colin
Neufeld, Sasa Radulovic, Shannon Wiebe
Location: Winnipeg, Manitoba
Area: 26,000 s.f.
Completion: 2009 (phase 1)
Construction: Boretta Construction
Structural: Hanuschak Consultants Inc.
Mechanical: G.D. Stasynec & Associates Ltd.
Landscape: Lynnette Postuma
Renderings: 5468796 Architecture Inc.

AGATHOM Co.

3 Gilead Place
Toronto, Ontario M5A 3C8
T 416 203 9068
F 416 203 9360
www.agathom.com
info@agathom.com

Molly's Cabin
Design team: Adam Thom, Katja Aga Sachse Thom
Location: Pointe au Baril, Ontario
Area: 1,000 s.f.
Completion: 2008
Construction: Brian Thorkildsen
Structural: Halcrow Yolles
Photography: Michael Awad, Paul Orenstein

Altius Architecture Inc.

One Atlantic Avenue #120
Toronto, Ontario M6K 3E7
T 416 516 7772
F 416 516 7774
www.altius.net
design@altius.net

Eels Lake Cottage
Design team: Trevor McIvor, Tony Round
Location: Apsley, Ontario
Area: 3,200 s.f.
Completion: 2007
Construction: Neal Brinkman & Sons,
with Altius Architecture Inc.
Structural: Blackwell Bowick Partnership
Mechanical/geothermal: Havencraft Homes
Photography: Patrick Burke, Tony Round

Campos Leckie

1730 Stephens Street
Vancouver, British Columbia V6K 3V6
T 604 734 1458
F 604 734 1424
www.camposleckie.ca
info@camposleckie.ca

Zacatitos 001
Design team: Javier Campos, Matthew Chan,
Henning Knötzele, Peeroj Thakre
Location: Baja California Sur, Mexico
Area: 3,100 s.f.
Completion: 2003
Construction: Ian McGonagle (Aguaclara S.A. de C.V.)
Structural: Francico Hernández Váldez, Alcabo
Photography: Javier Campos, Don Bull

D'Arcy Jones Design Inc.

204 - 175 East Broadway
Vancouver, British Columbia V5T 1W2
T 604 669 2235
F 604 669 2231
www.darcyjones.com
mail@darcyjones.com

Anderson House
Design team: D'Arcy Jones, Milos Begovic, Arya
Safavi, Amanda Kemeny
Location: Saltspring Island, British Columbia
Area: 1,500 s.f.
Completion: 2009
Construction: Alan McMaster with Strait
Construction Ltd.
Structural: Ennova Structural Engineering
Renderings: Arya Safavi

Ernst-Ongman House
Design team: D'Arcy Jones, Milos Begovic, Arya
Safavi, Amanda Kemeny
Location: Whistler, British Columbia
Area: 2,300 s.f.
Completion: 2009
Construction: Kris Ongman, Colin Ernst
Structural: Ennova Structural Engineering
Renderings: Arya Safavi

Dubbeldam Design Architects

401 Richmond Street West, Studio 258
Toronto, Ontario M5V 3A8
T 416 913 6757
F 416 913 6759
www.dubbeldamarchitects.com
design@dubbeldamarchitects.com

Cabbagetown Residence
Design team: Heather Dubbeldam, Tania
Ursomarzo, Katya Marshall, Heather Ross,
Katrina Touw
Location: Toronto, Ontario
Area: 2,300 s.f.
Completion: 2008
Construction: Troke Contracting
Structural: K.H. Davis Consulting Ltd.
Photography: Shai Gil

EVOKE International Design Inc.

2388 Alberta Street
Vancouver, British Columbia V5K 3K7
T 604 875 8667
F 604 875 1943
www.evoke.ca
studio@evoke.ca

W9 Houses
Design team: David Nicolay, Jake Smith, Pieter de
Bruin, Becki Chan
Location: Vancouver, British Columbia
Area: 2,000 s.f.
Completion: 2009
Construction: Linden Construction
Structural: Wicke Herfst Maver Structural
Engineers
Rendering: Tomas Machnikowski, Evoke

Gow Hastings Architects Inc.

51 Wolseley Street, 2nd Floor
Toronto, Ontario M5T 1A4
T 416 920 0031
F 416 920 0288
www.gowhastings.com
info@gowhastings.com

Humber Students' Federation
Design team: Philip Hastings,
Jim Burkitt, Janice Lee, Jimmy Sunn
Location: Toronto, Ontario
Area: 4,500 s.f.
Completion: 2008
Construction: Compass Construction Resources Ltd.
Structural: Halcrow Yolles
Mechanical/electrical: McGregor Allsop Ltd.
Photography: Tom Arban

Canadian Centre for Culinary Arts and Science
Design team: Philip Hastings, Valerie Gow, Hugo
Martins, Greg Demaiter, Katrina Touw, Janice Lee
Location: Toronto, Ontario
Area: 7,500 s.f.
Completion: 2008
Construction: Compass Construction Resources Ltd.
Structural: Robert E. Brown & Associates
Mechanical: Enso Systems Inc.
Electrical: DeCaria Engineering Ltd.
Food service: Cini-Little International
Photography: Tom Arban

Lapointe Architects

10 Saint Mary Street, Suite 606
Toronto, Ontario M4Y 1P9
T 416 964 6641
F 416 964 6643
www.lapointe-arch.com
info@lapointe-arch.com

Fifth Town Artisan Cheese Factory
Design team: Francis Lapointe, Paul Dolick, Kathy
Kurtz, Michael Del Puerto
Location: Prince Edward County, Ontario
Area: 4,600 s.f.
Completion: 2008
Construction: K. Knudsen Construction Ltd.
Structural: Blackwell Bowick Partnership
Environmental: Enermodal Engineering
Photography: Ben Rahn (A-Frame), Lapointe
Architects

Lateral Office

242 Concord Avenue
Toronto, Ontario M6H 2P5
T 416 534 9532
F 416 971 2094
www.lateralarch.com
lateral@lateralarch.com

Clearing
Design team: Mason White, Lola Sheppard,
Joseph Yau
Location: Toronto, Ontario
Area: –
Completion: 2008
Construction: Joseph Yau, Holly Jordan,
Richard Lam, Shane Neill, Virginia Fernandez
Photography: Peter Legris

From Runways to Greenways
Design team: Mason White, Lola Sheppard,
Neeraj Bhatia, Imola Berczi, Daniel Rabin, Valerie
Tam, Antoine Morris
Location: Reykjavik, Iceland
Area: –
Completion: 2008 (unbuilt)
Renderings: Lateral Office

Marko Simcic Architect

955 West 19th Avenue
Vancouver, British Columbia V5Z 1X6
T 604 731 3879
F 604 731 3899
www.markosimcic.com
info@markosimcic.com

South Pender Island Retreat
Design team: Marko Simcic, Brian Broster
Location: South Pender Island, British Columbia
Area: 2,500 s.f.
Completion: 2008
Construction: Stig Liljedahl
Structural: Ennova Structural Engineers
Photography: Marko Simcic Architect

Metchosin House
Design team: Marko Simcic, Brian Broster
Location: Metchosin, British Columbia
Area: 8,000 s.f.
Completion: 2006
Construction: Anderson Cove Construction
Structural: Equilibrium Consulting
Landscape: Maureen Smith,
id a Landscape Design
Arborist: Don Bottrell, Dogwood Tree Services
Agrologist: Robert Maxwell
Photography: Peter Powles, Marko Simcic Architect

mcfarlane | green | biggar
ARCHITECTURE + DESIGN

15 Chesterfield Place
North Vancouver, British Columbia V7M 3K3
T 604 908 9924
F 604 980 9915
www.mgb-architecture.ca
info@mgb-architecture.ca

Prince George Airport
Design team: Steve McFarlane, Michael Green
Location: Prince George, British Columbia
Area: 47,000 s.f.
Completion: 2005
Construction: Wayne Watson Construction Ltd
Structural: Equilibrium Consulting
Photography: mcfarlane | green | biggar
ARCHITECTURE + DESIGN

Obakki
Design team: Michelle Biggar, Michael Green
Location: Vancouver, British Columbia
Area: 5,500 s.f.
Completion: 2006
Construction: Artech Construction
Consultant: Brent Comber
Photography: Scott Morgan

_naturehumaine [architecture+design]

7458, rue Berri
Montréal, Québec H2R 2G5
T 514 273 6316
F 514 273 5510
www.naturehumaine.com
ma@naturehumaine.com

Quattro D
Design team: Marc-André Plasse, Stéphane
Rasselet, Emmanuelle Lapointe, Rebecca Wei
Location: Montréal, Québec
Area: 2,800 s.f.
Completion: 2007
Graphic designers : Studio FEED
(ceiling), Pastille Rose (identity)
Photography: _naturehumaine

Residence Garnier
Design team: Stéphane Rasselet, Emmanuelle
Lapointe, Marc-André Plasse
Location: Montréal, Québec
Area: 1,900 s.f.
Completion: 2008
Construction: NICORA
Photography: _naturehumaine

NIPpaysage

7468, rue Drolet
Montréal, Québec H2R 2C4
T 514 272 6626
F 514 272 6622
www.nippaysage.ca
nip@nippaysage.ca

Beaten Track
Design team: NIPpaysage
Location: Québec City, Québec
Area: 1,200 s.f.
Completion: 2008
Construction: Astuce Décor Inc.
Photography: Jacques Bourdages

Point Pleasant Park
Design team: NIPpaysage, Ekistics Planning
and Design
Location: Halifax, Nova Scotia
Area: 185 acres
Completion: 2008
Photography: NIPpaysage

Project Credits

North Design Office

45 Wright Avenue
Toronto, Ontario M6R 1K9
T 416 532 9875
F 416 532 8874
www.northdesignoffice.ca
pnorth@northdesignoffice.ca

The Verdant Walk

Design team: Pete North, Alissa North
Location: Cleveland, Ohio, USA
Area: 26,700 s.f.
Completion: 2008
Client Sponsor: Cleveland Public Art
Construction: Park Works Cleveland,
Eventscape, Blackwell Bowick, Ohio
Prairie Nursery, Carrick's Landscaping
Photography: North Design Office, Ryan Di Vita

Paul Raff Studio

204 Spadina Avenue, Suite 200
Toronto, Ontario M5T 2C2
T 416 365 7800
F 416 352 5954
www.paulraffstudio.com
studio@paulraffstudio.com

Cascade House

Design team: Paul Raff, Samantha Scroggie,
Rick Galazowski, Scott Barker, Jennifer Ujimoto,
Gillian Lazanik, Jean-Philipe Finkelstein, Adam
Thom, Jane Son
Location: Toronto, Ontario
Area: 3,500 s.f.
Completion: 2008
Construction: T Fijalkowski and Associates
Structural: Neumann Associates
Landscape: Scott Torrance Landscape Architect
Photography: Ben Rahn (A-Frame), Steve Tsai,
Paul Raff Studio

RVTR

204 Spadina Avenue, Suite 200
Toronto, Ontario M5T 2C2
T 416 219 5255
F –
www.rvtr.com
mail@rvtr.com

Post Carbon Highway

Design team: Kathy Velikov, Geoffrey Thün, Matt
Peddie, Matt Storus, Sonja Storey-Fleming
Location: Ontario, Great Lakes Megaregion
Area: 8,000 Ha
Duration: 2008 - 2011
Commissioning agents: SSHRC, University
of Michigan, Garner Enterprises
Renderings: RVTR

Latitude Housing System

Design team: Kathy Velikov, Geoffrey Thün, Colin
Ripley, Paul Raff, Matt Storus, Lauren Abrahams,
Maya Przybylski
Location: Cherepovets, Russia (and other cold
climate sites)
Area: 1,200 - 3,800 s.f.
Completion: 2009 (prototype)
Structural: Blackwell Bowick Partnership
Mechanical: Ecologix
Building science: Dr. John Straube
BIPV: Schuco USA, Day4Energy, Veissmann
Logistics: Thorax Design
Fabrication: MCM 2001 Inc.
Renderings: RVTR

spmb

207 Kingsway Avenue
Winnipeg, Manitoba R3M 0G4
T 204 774 8288
F 204 474 7533
www.spmb.ca
info@spmb.ca

Plage

Design team: Eduardo Aquino, Karen Shanski
Location: Québec City, Québec
Area: 1,550 s.f.
Completion: 2008
Construction: Carnaval de Québec (Daniel
Bouchard)
Sound: Ken Gregory
Photography: spmb

Table of Contents

Design team: Eduardo Aquino, Karen Shanski
Location: Winnipeg, Manitoba
Area: 1,030 s.f.
Completion: 2006
Construction: SCT Welding and Metal
Photography: William Eakin, spmb

Susan Fitzgerald Architecture

2061 Elm Street
Halifax, Nova Scotia B3L 2Y2
T 902 830 1024
F 902 422 3321
www.susanfitzgeraldarchitecture.com
susan@susanfitzgeraldarchitecture.com

26 Bridgeview Drive

Design team: Susan Fitzgerald
Location: Halifax, Nova Scotia
Area: 2,600 s.f.
Completion: 2008
Construction: Brainard Fitzgerald Developments
Structural: Andrea Doncaster
Photography: Jamie Steeves

2061 Elm Street

Design team: Susan Fitzgerald
Location: Halifax, Nova Scotia
Area: 1,800 s.f.
Completion: 2007
Construction: Brainard Fitzgerald Developments
Structural: Andrea Doncaster
Photography: Jamie Steeves

The Acre Collective

5 Westview Drive
Saint John, New Brunswick E2K 2G6
T 506 651 3647
F –
www.theacre.ca
monica@theacre.ca

Hapito

Design team: Mónica Adair, Stephen Kopp
Location: Saint John, New Brunswick
Area: 100 s.f.
Completion: 2007
Construction: Al & Curtis Fanjoy
Photography: Mark Hemmings, Stephen Kopp

Urban Republic arts society/
ph5 architecture inc.

#1- 155 Water Street
Vancouver, British Columbia V6B 1A7
T 604 605 1556
F 604 739 1991
www.urbanrepublic.ca
info@urbanrepublic.ca

The Gastown Drive-In

Design team: Henning Knoetzele, Peeroj Thakre
Location: Vancouver, British Columbia
Area: 33,800 s.f.
Completion: 2008
Scaffolding Construction: Wild Coast Productions
Film consultant: Michelle Bjornson
Film partner: Cineworks Independent Film Society
Structural: Read Jones Christoffersen
Consulting Engineers, Bogdonov Pao
Associates Consulting Structural Engineers
Electrical: Corrente Electric
Audio-visual: Woodhouse & Associates
Photography: Gavin Mackenzie

Essay Authors

Alex Bozikovic is an editor at *The Globe and Mail*. He has won two National Magazine Awards for his writing on architecture and design; he contributes to publications such as *Azure, Metropolis, Frame,* and *Dwell.*

David Theodore is a doctoral student in architecture and the history of science at Harvard University. He recently taught in Montréal in the School of Architecture, McGill University, as a research associate, and in the Department of Design, Concordia University. An active design journalist and critic, he serves as a regional correspondent for *The Canadian Architect*, is contributing editor at *Azure*, and was a contributor to the *Phaidon Atlas of 21st-Century World Architecture.*

Twenty + Change 02 Sponsors

Twenty + Change would like to thank the following sponsors who generously helped make this exhibition and publication possible.

Publication Sponsors

Canada Council for the Arts
Royal Architecture Institute of Canada

Supporting Sponsors

PCL Construction Leaders
Forbo Flooring Systems

Exhibition Print Sponsor

Astley Gilbert Limited

Exhibition Sponsors

Blackwell Bowick Partnership Limited
Dunleavy Cordun Associates Inc.
Fowler Bauld & Mitchell Architects
Ridley Windows and Doors Inc.
Velux Canada inc.

Manitoba Association of Architects
Nova Scotia Association of Architects
Architectural Institute of British Columbia

Festival of Architecture & Design
University of Waterloo School of Architecture

Gifts-in-kind

Gladstone Hotel
Barzelle Designs Ltd.

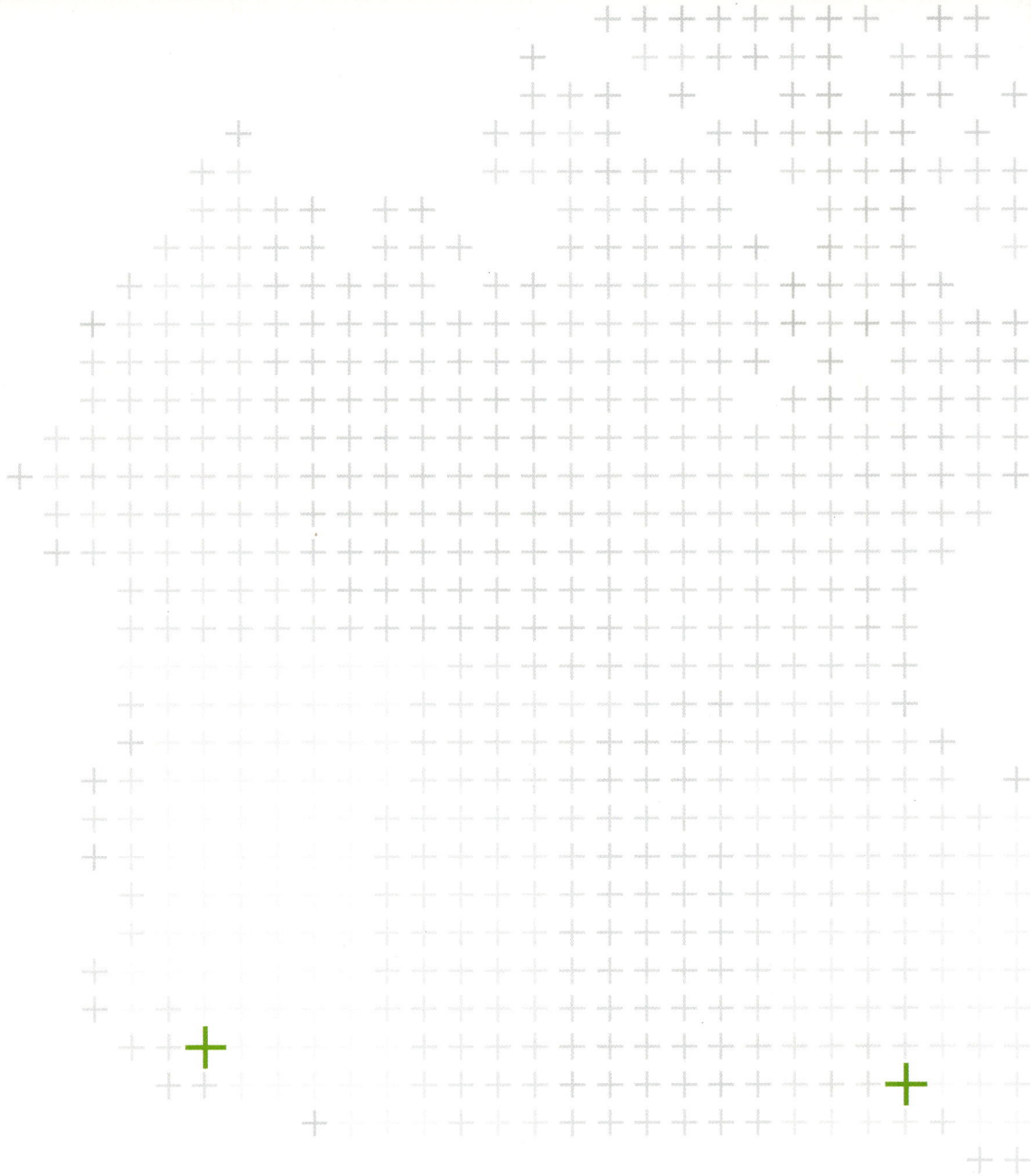